How the Inconceivable was Conceived:

Sinking the Church?

STEVE DONALD

DayOne

© Day One Publications 2024

ISBN 978-1-84625-787-2

All Scripture quotations, unless stated otherwise, are from the
anglicized edition of the ESV Bible copyright © 2002 Collins, part of
HarperCollins Publishers.

British Library Cataloguing in Publication Data available
Published by Day One Publications
Ryelands Road, Leominster, HR6 8NZ
Telephone 01568 613 740 FAX 01568 611 473
email—sales@dayone.co.uk
web site—www.dayone.co.uk

Cover design by Kathryn Chedgzoy
Printed by 4edge

Dedication
I would like to dedicate this book to my
son-in-law, Rev. Ben Graham, and to all the
faithful minsters of the gospel in his
generation.

Endorsements

The Church of England is living through perilous times, caused in part by tectonic shifts in popular culture and in part by lack of a clear direction in the Church itself. In this clarion call to action, Steve Donald outlines the process by which we have arrived at the current crisis and issues a stark warning that we must wake up and fight back with all the spiritual weapons at our disposal. He shows us that we must be faithful to Christ, obedient to his Word and clear in our convictions. We must love our enemies by declaring the truth and urging them to repent before it is too late. What nobody could have imagined half a century ago has now happened, and there is no time to waste. This book is a much-needed wake-up call to faithful Christians everywhere and a sign that God is stirring up new life among the embers of a dying society.

Gerald Bray, director of Research, Latimer Trust, London, formerly Research Professor of Divinity (history and doctrine), Beeson Divinity School, Samford, for over thirty years and the author of many books.

Acknowledgements

I am very grateful for the brilliant help I have received from Helen Clark at Day One. It has been a pleasure. Can I also thank Sue Carey, who read through the book and gave encouragement and helpful feedback, especially on Chapter 1 and on the title. Sue thought I must have the word, 'Inconceivable', in the title and helped me get there. I would like to thank Gerald Bray for his excellent commendation. Finally, I would like to thank Graham Stamford for his godly encouragement in our ministry together; as Proverbs 27:17 says, 'Iron sharpens iron, and one man sharpens another.' We are collaborating in developing Greatest Life Ministries: https://greatestlifeministries.com/our-team

Contents

1 Inconceivable

The problem of culture

Christians have a problem with culture—especially with the huge disconnect that has developed between the Church and the Western World in the last forty or fifty years. How are we to respond to these changes? Take the example of contemporary films and television. Christians may be shocked when ministers, such as myself, watch contemporary films—films which themselves reflect the culture in which we live. Of course, clearly toxic films and television series should be avoided because of their content. We must exercise discernment, but we must also engage with culture. We are to be in the world but not of it (John 17:16). While we are in the world, we need to have, as John Stott put it, 'one foot in the Biblical World and one in our culture',[1] otherwise we are in danger of losing connection with ordinary people and becoming withdrawn into a world only occupied by those who agree with us! If we are to be 'salt' and 'light' (Matthew 5:13–16) and give witness to Christ, then we must be engaged, and I would argue that watching films and television series can help us to understand the culture we live in. The apostle Peter wisely gives us the godly way we can do this, when he says in the opening phrase of 1 Peter 3:15:

> But in your hearts honour Christ the Lord as holy, always being prepared to make a defence to anyone who asks you for a reason for the hope that is in you; yet do it with gentleness and respect.

My wife, Gloria, and I used to enjoy watching films and then analysing them from a biblical point of view. One of our favourite films was *The Princess Bride* (1987), which is just a bit of heartwarming fun. Peter Cook plays 'The Impressive Clergyman' with a speech impediment. He presides over a marriage ceremony, shortened by the wicked Prince Humperdinck (Chris Sarandon) because Westley (Cary Elwes), the true love of Buttercup (Robin Wright), is about to storm the castle to save her from his wicked clutches. Peter Cook says, 'Have you the wing?' (He meant 'ring'.) The whole film is full of such memorable phrases and words!

Earlier in the film, a Spaniard (Mandy Patinkin) and Fezzik (Andre the Giant) are employed and led by Vizzini (Wallace Shawn) to kidnap Buttercup for the Prince. Vizzini pronounces what he is witnessing as 'Inconceivable!' on four separate occasions. He watches Westley follow in a sailboat through choppy, giant-snake-infested waters, climb an impossible rock face and successfully overcome the Spaniard and the Giant in one-on-one combat to save Buttercup. Westley then challenges Vizzini, who is holding Buttercup prisoner with a dagger at her throat, to a dual to the death: to a battle of wits by deciding which one of two goblets Westley has put poison in. Vizzini considers himself cleverer than Plato or Socrates and is confident he can outthink Westley and choose the poison-free goblet by his superior intellect and win the lethal contest. Westley, cleverly, has put an entirely fictional poison iocaine in each goblet, outsmarting Vizzini because, over time, using lesser amounts of the poison, Westley has built up an immunity from its lethal effects. Both men drink from their goblets of wine and Vizzini at once falls down dead, while Westley walks away, showing no ill effects.

There are no great philosophical or theological themes in the film, *The Princess Bride*, but it is very entertaining, especially Vizzini's repetition of the word, 'Inconceivable', which brings me back to the theme of this book!

The conceiving of the inconceivable

There is a huge majority in the wider Anglican Communion and a sizeable number in the Church of England who find the recent votes in the General Synod as 'inconceivable'. They were shocked by the decision in the February 2023 Synod to continue looking at how same-sex blessing could be introduced and, by the November Synod, to authorize a trial period of same-sex blessings in the Church of England. These votes were led by the House of Bishops. Bishops in New Zealand and Australia have already adopted this innovation against the clear teaching of the Bible. Historically, the Church of England is the mother church to the Anglican Communion, from which Anglican missionaries took the gospel to the far-flung parts of the former British Empire—places like Africa, South-East Asia, Australia, and North and South America. Embracing this sinful act as holy, marks a passing the point of no return for orthodox Anglicans, who make up 75% of Anglicans globally (their total number is 80 million.

Persecution is to be avoided at all costs (?) and false teaching is to be tolerated and even embraced (?) so we can 'go along to get along'(?).

In this book, I would like to explore the premise that while persecution does not destroy the church, false teaching certainly does, and therefore argue that the latter must be resisted. If the ark is the church, and the sea is the world, then if the sea gets into the boat it begins to sink. This has been happening in the Church of England over the last forty years, culminating in the recent decisions by the General Synod, led by the House of Bishops. I also want to explore the tension between how we understand the sovereignty of God—for, as Jesus says, 'I will build my church and the gates of hell shall not prevail against it,' (Matthew 16:18)—and our knowledge of the very human aspect of church life: namely that the church is weak, erring and, at times, despairing.

Recognition of the spiritual battle is critical.

Another important dimension is the recognition of a spiritual battle that we are called to enter, while trusting in the strength of God. The apostle Paul addresses this in Ephesians 6:10–11: 'Be strong in the Lord and in the strength of his might. Put on the whole armour of God.' This will be discussed in Chapter 2. We will see that, where the church is prepared to suffer and engage in this spiritual warfare, it is growing rapidly and where it does not stand up for Christ and face the inevitable suffering, it withers and dies.

We will see, in Chapter 3, that what Bishop Ryle called, 'Jellyfish Christianity', is killing the Church of England. Throughout the book, we will reflect on our present struggle, particularly in the Anglican Church in England, in the light of Paul's dying epistle to his son in the faith in 2 Timothy. The Church there, humanly speaking, was facing annihilation; Timothy felt his weakness and Paul was deeply concerned for him. And yet, through the power and sovereignty of God, the Church prevailed despite false teaching and persecution. Something similar faced the Church in the West, when the Roman Empire collapsed and Europe entered a so-called 'dark age'. God preserved his Church through people like Saint Benedict. Commentators, like Rod Dreher, suggest we are facing a cultural storm of comparable size ourselves. How can the living Church in England survive and eventually overcome?

Forty years of liberal drift

The tragedy we are seeing unfold has been a long time coming. The Church of England has finally turned away from the Lord. Chapter 4 outlines forty years of liberal drift in the Church of England. The decision to endorse gay blessings by the Church of England has once again torn the fabric of the Anglican Communion, as it did with the consecration of the first gay bishop, Gene Robinson, by the American Episcopal Church in 2005. Since then, same-sex blessings have gone ahead in the Church of Wales and gay marriage in the Scottish Episcopal Church, but now for the Church of England to do this is incredibly significant.

In 2008, the Global Anglican Future Conference (GAFCON) was set up by national archbishops (known as Primates in the Anglican Communion) in direct response to the consecration of the first gay bishop. At the 4th GAFCON in Kigali, Rwanda, in April 2023, the response to the decision of the Church of England to go ahead with same-sex blessings was a decision to no longer acknowledge the Archbishop of Canterbury as 'the first among equals' within the Anglican Primates.

When I attended the 2nd GAFCON, held in 2014 in Nairobi, Kenya, along with the English delegation, we were keen to tell those in the persecuted Anglican Churches how much we felt for them and were praying for them. The general reaction to this was for them to tell us they were thankful for our prayers, but they were far more concerned about the liberal drift in the Church of England than their own sufferings! In 2014, the signs were there of a steady move away from the authority of the Bible, but what has happened this year in the General Synod shows that the point of no return has been passed.

Paul's dying epistle gives insight and hope.

At the end of his life and ministry, the apostle Paul declared, 'all who are in Asia turned away from me' (2 Timothy 1:15). This, too, was surely inconceivable. Paul was facing imminent death and the apparent failure of the gospel at the time. Throughout this book, we shall draw upon Paul's last epistle, 2 Timothy, because it is about gospel faithfulness and hope in the face of physical persecution and suffering:

> I have fought the good fight, I have finished the race, I have kept the faith. Henceforth there is laid up for me the crown of righteousness, which the Lord, the righteous judge, will award to me on that Day, and not only to me but also to all who have loved his appearing (2 Timothy 4:7–8).

The second letter to Timothy shows that while physical persecution does not destroy the church (Tertullian, one of the early church fathers stated: 'The blood of the martyrs is the seed of the Church'),[2] false teaching always does.

Speaking of Dr Martyn Lloyd-Jones, Sinclair Ferguson wrote:

> Like the early fathers of the church, he well knew that not even

physical persecution can destroy the Church of Jesus Christ, but false teaching always will.[3]

When the sea (the world) gets into the ark (the church), the ark sinks!

Chapter 5 will show how false ideas have entered the church like the sea entering a sinking ship! How and why has this massive change happened in the Church of England? False teaching, which Paul says, 'will spread like gangrene' (2 Timothy 2:17–18), has undermined the authority of the Bible and, therefore, the biblical gospel. This book will seek to map out the underlying forces and ideas that have taken over much of the Western Church over the last forty years and will trace back these ideas to influential thinkers like Rousseau, Marx, and Freud. Together with this, I will work through my own practical experience over several decades as a vicar in the Church of England, and I believe this will all help to explain how we got where we are. Of course, the authority of the Bible has also been eroded in the Free Church as well.

Why is the issue of homosexuality church-defining?

You could ask why the Global Anglican Future Conference (GAFCON)—along with the Global South who make up 75% of the 80 million Anglicans in the world—focuses so much on this issue of homosexuality? Their response reveals two competing world views, and this will become more apparent in Chapter 6: 'Discerning truth and Error'. There we will look at the recent papers written by the Bishop of Oxford, Steven Croft, in favour of same-sex blessings and the response from one of his clergy, Vaughan Roberts, Rector of St

Ebbs, Oxford, who is himself same-sex attracted and who opposes this change to the Church of England's doctrine. These two world views offer two competing 'gospels' (one has a big G one a small g ?!) each claiming to offer hope and transformation.

Cultural Marxism and the undermining of biblical doctrine

Sharing personal details and examples will ground the description of the liberal drift in the Church of England with the real-life experience of a parish vicar. I have been involved in the Anglican Church for over forty years, firstly as a lay leader and then as an ordained clergyman for thirty-four years in four dioceses. I have seen how these ideas have taken over the establishment of the Church of England little by little, through what is known as Cultural Marxism combined with post-modernism in the secular culture and then, how it began affecting the Church of England. This is explored in Chapter 7. These ideas have now spread to every part of the Western Church, where the traditional teaching of the Bible on sexual ethics is scorned as toxic, repressive, and dogmatic by Liberal Progressives. The seeds of this go back many years.

When I went to the Anglican selection conference in 1986, my local vicar—who is now a retired liberal bishop—referred to me in a reference to the panel as 'dogmatic'. Carl Truman writes that, 'Christianity, as both Martin Luther and John Henry Newman knew, is dogmatic, doctrinal and assertive.'[4] Failure to hold onto the biblical doctrines with courage and resist the virus of what has become known as a 'woke'[5] mindset, has led to a catastrophic decline in mainline denominations. In contrast, church fellowships that are growing in England are those that hold to the authority of

Scripture and offer a welcome to all with clear teaching on sexual identity, marriage, and singleness.

Facing the sack, for sticking to the plain teaching of Scripture

I can give specific examples of the drift away from the authority of the Bible in the Church of England. During my time as a vicar, I witnessed many bishops adopting revisionist theologies; I attended compulsory clergy training offering a seminar entitled, 'alternative sexualities' in one diocese; and in another I was faced with the threat of dismissal by my diocesan bishop for refusing the ministry of an assistant bishop who told me 'he supported the ordination of homosexuals'. We would have accepted another bishop from the diocese for our parish confirmation, one who did believe in the sound teaching of Scripture, but the four bishops in the diocese closed ranks and put pressure on me to back down. This I refused to do since, as I told the diocesan bishop, it was a question of conscience before God, who would judge both me and him on the Day of Judgement (Romans 14:10–12.)

In the end, at my request, the diocesan bishop signed Lambeth 1:10 (a motion passed overwhelmingly in 1998 by the Anglican Communion which said that 'homosexual practice was incompatible with Scripture') and then, I was able to invite him to do the parish confirmation. In my last parish, from which I retired on Easter Day, 2022, the bishop officially supported traditional marriage and yet voted for same-sex blessings at the General Synod—based on putting unity first! Ecumenism, that stresses unity at the expense of orthodox biblical truth, was the only explanation for this behaviour, which I find quite shocking!! On hearing this, an Evangelical Free Church friend of mine exclaimed: 'Inconceivable!'

False teaching by its bishops is sinking the Church of England.

'Inconceivable!' aptly describes the sexual revolution in the church. In one sense it is hard to believe where we are and how quickly we arrived at this place but mapping the issue over forty years enables a view of the steady *liberal progressive* drift of the Church of England away from the authority of Scripture. We will see that ecumenism, with its belief that truth is trumped by unity, has been the handmaiden of false teaching. Bishops of the Church of England wrongly claim that they have received new revelation on the meaning of Scripture as they gather, and that unity is more important than doctrine. They have turned away from the plain teaching of Scripture and from the godly pastors and doctors of the Church through the ages. This liberal drift is not only important for the Church of England. Free Church friends tell me that what happens in the Church of England is important for them and for Christianity in the UK. This sexual revolution has deeply affected all the mainline denominations who are in severe decline, while churches who stick to the Bible are thriving.

The seeds planted by progressive liberal thinkers years ago have perverted the grace of God in the church. The pace at which this revolution has taken place is astounding. Why has the Church in the West been so powerless to resist acceptance of what amounts to another gospel and an alternative religion to Christianity? We will discover that seeds planted by liberal thinkers hundreds of years ago have entered the mainstream church through academia and the media and have gradually eaten away confidence in the sufficiency and authority of the Scriptures. The Church in the West has turned away from the truth and, as Jude, vv. 3–4 says:

> Beloved, although I was very eager to write to you about our common salvation, I found it necessary to write appealing to you to contend for the faith that was once for all delivered to the saints. For certain people have crept in unnoticed who long ago were designated for this condemnation, ungodly people, who pervert the grace of our God into sensuality and deny our only Master and Lord, Jesus Christ.

How loving is it to lead people to hell?

Liberal progressives stress the love of God, while rejecting the judgement of God on sin. By accepting same-sex blessing, they have perverted the grace of God into sensuality and deny the Lordship of Christ through his Word. This is a first order gospel issue on at least two counts. Firstly, if sin is no longer sin, then why did Christ die? Secondly, homosexual acts cause people to lose the Kingdom of God (1 Corinthians 6:9–11) and so, by deceiving them that this lifestyle is godly, false teachers are potentially sending them to hell! (How loving is that?!).

Let me give an important caveat at this point. What Paul says, in 1 Corinthians 6, includes other lifestyle choices that reflect unrighteousness (v. 9); a range of sexual sins, not just homosexuality, is mentioned—and also thieves, the greedy, drunkards, swindlers etc (v. 10). To this he could have added the self-righteous! As John Newton said, 'I am a great sinner and

Christ is a great Saviour,'[6] and that applies to everyone without exception. However, we are dealing with the specific issue of homosexuality here, and the Bible is clear that it is a sin to live in this way. If we choose to persist along this path without repentance and new life in Christ, we will lose our souls on Judgement Day. To 'go along to get along', as many clergy do, is to perpetuate a dangerous lie. Furthermore, if the church turns away from the Lordship of Christ and obedience to his revealed truth, then the Holy Spirit will leave the Church of England and all that will remain will be an aging congregation looking after decaying buildings.

Chapter 8 explores the future direction of our fast-changing culture and asks whether it will be more like the dystopian culture imagined by Orwell in his book, *1984*, or more like Huxley's *Brave New World*. Is it conceivable that there might be physical persecution of the confessional Church in England by the institutional church, using the state?

Chapter 9 recognizes from 2 Timothy and the history of the church, that God not man has the last word and asks what we need to think about to survive the present and ever-coming cultural storm. We will see that we need to accept the seriousness of the situation, hold to our credal beliefs, and build arks of community.

NOTES

1 Stott, John, *The Contemporary Christian: An Urgent Plea for Double Listening*, (Nottingham: IVP, 1992), pp. 101–113.

2 www.desiringgod.org/articles/the-seeds-none-could-afford

3 Ferguson, Sinclair, Cited in: Meyer, Jason, *Lloyd-Jones on the Christian Life*, (Wheaton, Illinois: Crossway Books, 2018), Foreword.

4 Trueman, Carl R., *The Rise and Triumph of the Modern Self*, (Wheaton, Illinois: Crossway, 2020), p. 403.

5 See Glossary of Terms at the back of this book for a definition.

6 John Newton full quote: "My memory is nearly gone, but I remember two things: that I am a great sinner, and that Christ is a great Saviour." Bull, Josiah, *'But now I see': The Life of John Newton*, (Carlisle: The Banner of Truth Trust, 1998), p. 358.

2 A call to spiritual warfare

The Christian life is like a tightrope.

In this chapter, I want to ask why, and in what way are we 'to contend for the faith that was once for all delivered to the saints'? (Jude v. 3). There are powerful voices telling us we should not rock the boat and that we should put away concerns about doctrinal faithfulness and clarity for the sake of the unity of the church. There are other powerful voices telling us to resist and fight the good fight. But what is a good fight? The Christian life is like walking a tightrope and it is easy to fall off on one side or the other. Dr Martyn Lloyd-Jones, in his book, *The Christian Soldier: An Exposition of Ephesians 6:10–20*, has some excellent advice in order to get the balance right. Firstly, he asserts:

> It is a very difficult matter, because we are told two things in the Scriptures. First of all, we are exhorted to 'contend earnestly for the faith'. That is Jude's exhortation ... And there is great need of this at this present time ...There are some people who never defend the faith at all. They claim they are just nice, good people, who do not argue, who do not understand, who are not 'controversialists'.[1]

Lloyd-Jones is unequivocal, when he concludes: 'That is an unscriptural position to assume for we are meant to contend earnestly for the faith.' I have been told many times I should not contend, but this is an unscriptural and cowardly approach. However, there are spiritual dangers to our souls and those of others if we enter into controversy in the wrong spirit.

If we are to contend for the faith, as Christians how should we do it?
What is the good fight? How do we stay on the tightrope and not fall off?

Under a chapter heading of 'Things to Avoid', Martyn Lloyd-Jones warns of 'dissipation of energy' and that 'many a man has become weak who was once strong, simply because he was over-exerting himself in many ways ... losing the edge of their spiritual lives'.[2] I was in danger of this very thing when leading a sizeable church with a staff team; I felt I had to contend nationally and locally over the homosexual issue within the Church of England. Over time, I was losing my spiritual edge and ended up quite exhausted. On top of this, I was faced with a transexual issue in the church leadership that nearly broke me and my wife, Gloria, partly due to a lack of support from my church leaders. I believe I was taking the right approach, but I had taken my eyes off Jesus and adopted 'striving' rather than 'resting'. I got to the point where I was no longer able to function properly as a minster and was close to a nervous breakdown; I had to take an emergency sabbatical from parish life. It was right for me to contend but over time I had succumbed to 'striving' instead of resting in the Lord and his mighty strength. We must contend but not strive, says Lloyd-Jones. We see several warnings of the wrong approach in 2 Timothy:

- Chapter 2:14: 'Remind them of these things, and charge them before God not to quarrel about words, which does no good, but only ruins the hearers.'
- Chapter 2:23–25: 'Have nothing to do with foolish, ignorant controversies; you know that they breed quarrels. And the Lord's servant must not be quarrelsome but kind to everyone,

able to teach, patiently enduring evil, correcting his opponents with gentleness.'

Discerning the right approach

Lloyd-Jones gives us excellent advice that seeks a biblical balance:

> The test of everything must always be whether it is profitable — profitable to our own souls, profitable to the souls of other people … 'Striving' means that your spirit is wrong, and once your spirit is wrong your motive becomes wrong … At one and the same time we have to contend for the faith and to refrain from striving.[3]

With God's grace, and a change of parish, I was able to recover my spiritual health and contend without striving.

So, there is a scriptural call for all true Christians to wage spiritual warfare against sin, the world and the devil. We forget at our spiritual peril that both our Lord Jesus and the apostle Paul were controversialists who contended for the truth against error. Early on in my ministry, the Lord laid on me verses from 1 Timothy 1:18–20 that, by the grace and strength of God, I have kept as a watchword for my soul:

> This charge I entrust to you, Timothy, my child, in accordance with the prophecies previously made about you, that by them you may wage the good warfare, holding faith and a good conscience. By rejecting this, some have made shipwreck of their faith, among whom are Hymenaeus and Alexander, whom I have handed over to Satan that they may learn not to blaspheme.

I can testify to my own struggles to be faithful to my ordination vows, as I have already mentioned. I am to repent continually of my own sin and seek the transforming power of the Holy Spirit and the Word of God. I am also to engage in spiritual warfare, as Paul expresses it in Ephesians 6:10: 'Finally, be strong in the Lord and in the strength of his might.' This means a continual dependence on God to overcome evil and a passion to teach and live a holy life. I do this by 'holding on to faith and a good conscience'.

At my ordination service in Chester Cathedral in 1988, the bishop asked, '*Will* you be ready, with all faithful diligence, to banish and drive away all erroneous and strange doctrines contrary to God's Word; and to use both public and private warnings and exhortations?' I answered, 'I will, the Lord being my helper.' When bishops fail to feed and protect the flock of God as they promised at their consecration, it falls to the rest of the clergy and laity to call them to repentance by 'public and private warnings and exhortations'. When ferocious wolves enter the sheep pen as bishops and vicars, it is the duty of all faithful pastors to resist them and warn the sheep (publicly and privately) of the danger to their souls (Acts 20:29–30).

The moving of tectonic plates

It is clear that the vast majority of worldwide Anglicans have been shocked and appalled by the decision of the Church of England Synod to permit same-sex blessings. However, the response has expressed a deeply felt desire to reset the Anglican Communion on a sound Biblical basis. The Kigali GAFCON 4 represents 'a moving of the tectonic plates for Anglicanism', says George Conger who attended on behalf of *Anglican Unscripted*—a popular show on a well-known video sharing platform that covers Anglican news once a week.[4]

Instead of being a political movement responding to the errors of Primates such as the Archbishop of Canterbury and his errant bishops, there is a new dawn, shedding the colonial past where the head of the Anglican Communion was appointed by the British prime minister and moving to a new era where the Anglican Communion resets in a spiritual way its own future and its own structures with absolute confidence in the clear teaching of the Bible. Archbishop Foley Beach, chair of GAFCON, issued a call for repentance for all believers, beginning with GAFCON members. This is a typically Anglican way since most Anglican services begin with repentance before God and man.

Archbishop Ben Kwashi, GAFCON secretary, followed this with the announcement of the target of $10 million for a decade of evangelism and discipleship, not politics. Priorities would include young people, social outreach, and seminarians in places like Pakistan. Instead of being in a political fight with Canterbury, GAFCON becomes a mission agency and Canterbury an irrelevance, unless it repents of false teaching. This shows a marked contrast between the two, with GAFCON focusing on a Confessing Communion based on the plain teaching of Scripture, and the Canterbury Communion defined by an outdated institution that has lost the gospel.

The other major body representing the orthodox Anglican Primates, the Global South, has now decided to work much more closely with GAFCON and shares the same theology and aims but differs on approach. There will be no merger for now. Before any formal split with Canterbury, the Global South must deal with the fact that most Provinces had their legal constitutions drafted by English lawyers and English law, and it will take some time to hold a conference with members in order to redraft them, based on confessional orthodoxy rather than loyalty to a redundant and failing Canterbury institution.

To go or to stay?

Meanwhile, this leaves orthodox Anglicans who remain in the Church of England structures, like my son-in-law, in a difficult place, while others have chosen to leave the Church of England and join GAFCON-supported parallel structures like the Anglican Mission in England (AMiE is part of the Anglican Network in Europe (ANiE), which was itself authorised as an irregular* Anglican structure in 2020 by the archbishops of GAFCON). The bigger Anglican Evangelical Churches like All Soul's, Langham Place, where John Stott was rector for many years, and St Helen's Bishopsgate and St Ebb's in Oxford who have stayed in the Church of England, have stated that they are looking at ways of 'differentiation' and suspending payment of monies to the diocese in the short term, unless there is repentance. After a meeting with two hundred concerned evangelical clergy in the Diocese of London, the Bishop of London called an emergency finance meeting shortly afterwards.

Money is a gospel issue and parishes like Jesmond Parish Church in Newcastle and Christ Church Fulwood in Sheffield, while also staying in the Church of England, have long channelled funds away from liberal-diocesan coffers to help poorer churches and for church planting. In 1995, Christ Church Fulwood gave £100,000 towards a £320,000 new church building for St Andrews, Kendray, Barnsley, where I was the first vicar. The differences of approach between GAFCON and the Global South mirrors what is happening in evangelical Anglican Churches on the ground in England. Thousands of Anglican clergy and laity have believed it right to stay within the structures of the Church of England, (very much the Global South approach), while others (a much smaller but steadily growing group) have left and formed new Anglican structures outside the Church of England (very much the GAFCON approach). The challenge is for these loyal Anglicans to work together and see what comes out of discussions between the Archbishop of Canterbury and evangelical Anglican leaders in the near future.

A third non-geographical Province,[5] dismissed by the Church of England in the past, may again be in the mix when the majority of dioceses go financially belly-up, as evangelical money goes instead to orthodox mission in the UK. The bishops of the Church of England still hold all the power in relation to licensing clergy and so they would have to allow a third Province to have its own bishops who would licence their own clergy, and have their own theological education, safeguarding etc. This, they are unlikely to agree to unless there is overwhelming financial pressure.

How should orthodox Christians respond to the sexual revolution?
Carl Truman, in his book, *The Rise and Triumph of the Modern Self*, offers three suggestions to the Western Church: firstly, to acknowledge the serious nature of the threat to the Church in the

West because of the radical shift in culture; secondly, to hold onto its core beliefs; and thirdly, to build community.[6] As orthodox Anglican believers in England face the point of no return by the General Synod and either choose to remain within existing Church of England structures for now or in new structures outside them, they would do well to apply the points Truman makes.

What has happened was certainly inconceivable even ten years ago, but we must live in the real world, with God-given faith and courage, to seek a reset of the structures, while continuing the work of the gospel in growing churches, as GAFCON 4 has indicated. If this happens and we experience something of the growth that is happening in 75% of the Anglican communion (with persecutions), there will be much to thank God for, as a mission to reach England with the one true gospel becomes an exciting reality. This will require partnership with those who stay in the present Anglican structures and those Anglicans who decide to work outside it, as well as faithful, Free Church brothers and sisters in other church networks.

Such a reality may appear inconceivable given our parlous present state but for God nothing is impossible. God has brought reformation and revival to his Church in the past and he can do it again (Hebrews 13:8). What we are seeing in the present is a transitional phase, when our prayers should be that all faithful Christians in the UK will unite in a vision, with God's help, for the evangelization of the United Kingdom and the building up of his Church. True Christians love Jesus and want everyone to hear the good news and this focus on mission rather than church politics, given by the recent GAFCON meeting at Kigali, has the potential to be a spiritual game-changer for the UK and for the Anglican Communion. We live in demanding but exciting days when all true Christians in the UK need to step up to the plate and play their part. What has happened in The Church of England in the last forty years may be 'Inconceivable', but God is doing a new and wonderful thing, which gives hope for the future:

> Behold, I am doing a new thing; now it springs forth, do you not perceive it? I will make a way in the wilderness and rivers in the desert (Isaiah 43:19).

Building new arks

In the next chapter, we will examine how false teaching has been able to gain such a hold on the Church of England and set this within the wider collapse of the Western Church. If the ark is the church and the world is the ocean, then the ark is sinking because the ocean is getting into the ark! We are meant to be in the world, but not part of it. We need to build new arks—communities of local faithful believers—still in the world but not of it, committed to the Lord and his Word and to one another. We are not meant to be striving but resting in the power of the risen and ascended Christ while we build up the Church, contend for the faith and reach out in mission to a needy culture.

NOTES

1 Lloyd-Jones, D. Martyn, *The Christian Soldier: An Exposition of Ephesians 6:10–20*, (Edinburgh: Banner of Truth Trust, 1977), p. 144.

2 Ibid., p. 141.

3 Ibid., pp. 144–145.

4 https://www.youtube.com/watch?v=XDw_DkpERW4

5 The two existing Anglican Provinces in England are York in the north and Canterbury in the south. Diocese form part of each Province.

6 Truman, Carl, *The Rise and Triumph of the Modern Self*, (Wheaton, Illinois: Crossway, 2020), pp. 402–404.

3 Jellyfish Christianity

Doctrine matters.

How did the Church of England (the example we are using of the Western Church) arrive at the 'inconceivable' position described in the earlier chapters? To pick up the analogy of the first chapter, the ocean (the world) has got into the ark and caused it to sink. Why has this happened? Because false teaching has entered the church. Surely, it must also be due in part to the weakness of orthodox believers in the Church of England? They have let doctrine slip. Orthodox Christian, Rod Dreher's hope is:

> ... to wake up the church [the Western Church of which the Church of England is a part] and to encourage it to strengthen itself, while there is still time. If we want to survive, we have to return to the roots of our faith, both in thought and practice ... In short, we are going to be the church without compromise, no matter what it costs.'[1]

We need a return to doctrinal faithfulness. Rod Dreher authored his book, *The Benedict Option*, based on the prediction of cultural collapse of the Church in the West by the philosopher, Alasdair MacIntyre, who thinks the culture war is already lost. Traditionalists need to build arks to survive the storm that is already here and prepare for better days, just as in the 6th century, when Benedict devised his simple rule for the church to hold onto orthodox belief, as the Roman Empire folded.

Gospel faithfulness involves suffering.

Paul, in 2 Timothy, is facing the collapse of the church in his day that he had worked so hard to build up, amid widespread desertion. The second letter to Timothy is about gospel loyalty and the temptation to settle for a quiet life as a Christian. Paul gives Timothy encouragement to be faithful to the gospel despite suffering, as 1:7 shows: 'For God gave us a spirit not of fear but of power and love and self-control.' Paul's argument is not based on something like Prince Harry's *Invictus Games*, where the whole emphasis is on the triumph of the human spirit along.

Paul's whole argument begins with verse 8: 'Therefore do not be ashamed of the testimony about our Lord, nor of me his prisoner, but share in suffering for the gospel by the power of God,' and ends with verse 14: 'By the Holy Spirit who dwells within us, guard the good deposit entrusted to you.' We are to stand firm in our faith in Christ and there is a vital part for us to play but in the power of God, as we saw in the last chapter. We feel the emotional intensity at the beginning of the letter, when Paul writes to his spiritual son, Timothy: 'You are aware that all who are in Asia turned away from me' (2 Timothy 1:15). Will Timothy and the other Christians in the early church stick with Paul and his gospel or will they compromise for a more comfortable life? Will they display gospel loyalty despite suffering? Or, to repeat Rod Dreher's challenging words for today's Western Church:

> If we want to survive, ... we are going to be the church without compromise, no matter what it costs.

I love this quote which is attributed to Martin Luther. However, although this is not exactly what he said, the sentiments are the same:

> If I profess, with the loudest voice and clearest exposition, every portion of the truth of God except precisely that little point which the world and the devil are at that moment attacking, I am not confessing Christ, however boldly I may be professing Him. Where the battle rages, there the loyalty of the soldier is proved; and to be steady on all the battle front besides, is mere flight and disgrace if he flinches at that point.[2]

Jackals among the ruins

We have examples of faithless ministers in Ezekiel 13:1–6, 10:

> The word of the LORD came to me: 'Son of man, prophesy against the prophets of Israel, who are prophesying, and say to those who prophesy from their own hearts: "Hear the word of the LORD!" Thus says the LORD God, Woe to the foolish prophets who follow their own spirit, and have seen nothing! Your prophets have been like jackals among ruins, O Israel. You have not gone up into the breaches, or built up a wall for the house of Israel, that it might stand in battle in the day of the LORD. They have seen false visions and lying divinations. They say, "Declares the LORD", when the LORD has not sent them, and yet they expect him to fulfil their word … they have misled my people, saying, "Peace", when there is no peace.'

There are church leaders today who are like 'jackals among ruins'—strong words! We have seen these jackals in the support of a liberal agenda in the Church of England for over forty years, culminating in the adoption of same-sex blessings by the General

Synod in February 2023. Paul speaks of such leaders at a thriving church at Ephesus (Acts 20:28–31):

> Pay careful attention to yourselves and to all the flock, of which the Holy Spirit has made you overseers, to care for the church of God, which he obtained with his own blood. I know that after my departure fierce wolves will come in among you, not sparing the flock; and from among your own selves will arise men speaking twisted things, to draw away the disciples after them. Therefore be alert, remembering that for three years I did not cease night or day to admonish everyone with tears.

Pauls words show us that a faithful minister of the gospel both feeds the flock but also warns and protects the sheep from the wolves in sheep's clothing (see the warning of Jesus in Matthew 7:15–16!).

Bishop Ryle's warning about jellyfish Christianity

Bishop J. C. Ryle, who lived in Victorian times, warned of the effect on society and the church when biblical doctrine falls out of favour in the church. We end up, he predicted, with a 'jellyfish Christianity'. The following sadly could have been written of the 21st century:

> Eighteen centuries ago the apostle Paul forewarned us, 'The time will come when men will not put up with sound doctrine. Instead, to suit their own desires, they will gather around them a great number of teachers to say what their itching ears want to hear!' 2 Timothy 4:3 …
>
> The consequences of this widespread dislike to doctrine are very serious in the present day. Whether we like to allow it or not, it is an epidemic which is doing great harm. It creates, fosters, and keeps up an immense amount of instability in religion. It produces what I must

venture to call, if I may coin the phrase, a jellyfish Christianity in the churches—that is, a Christianity without bone, or muscle, or power.

A jellyfish, as everyone knows who has been much by the seaside, is a pretty and graceful object when it floats in the sea, contracting and expanding like a little, delicate, transparent umbrella. Yet the same jellyfish, when cast on the shore—is a mere helpless lump, without capacity for movement, self-defence, or self-preservation.

Alas! It is a vivid type of much of the religion of this day, of which the leading principle is, 'No dogma, no distinct tenets, no positive doctrine.'

We have hundreds of jellyfish clergymen, who seem not to have a single bone in their body of divinity. They have no definite opinions—they belong to no school or party. They are so afraid of 'extreme views'—that they have no views at all.

We have thousands of jellyfish sermons preached every year— sermons without an edge or a point. They are as smooth as billiard balls—awakening no sinner and edifying no saint.

We have legions of jellyfish young men annually turned out from our seminaries, armed with a few scraps of second-hand philosophy, who think it a mark of cleverness and intellect to have no decided opinions about anything in religion, and to be utterly unable to make up their minds as to what Christian truth is. Their proud hearts are not satisfied with truths which satisfied the godly of former years. Their only creed is a kind of 'Anythingism'. They believe everything— and are sure and positive about nothing!

And last, and worst of all, we have myriads of jellyfish worshipers— respectable church-going people, who have no distinct and definite views about any point in theology. They cannot discern things that differ, any more than colour-blind people can distinguish colours! They think that...

- everybody is right—and nobody is wrong,
- everything is true—and nothing is false,

- all sermons are good—and none are bad,
- every minister is sound—and none are unsound.

They are 'tossed to and fro, like children, by every wind of doctrine!' They are often carried away by any new excitement and sensational movement. They are ever ready for new things, because they have no firm grasp on the old Scripture truths.[3]

Doctrine matters and false teaching destroys the church, even if physical persecution does not. Bible-believing churches in the UK should be awake to the spiritual battle, and see 'the jackals among the ruins', and go 'up to the breaches in the wall to repair it for the people of Israel so that it will stand firm in the battle on the day of the LORD' (Ezekiel 13:5). If they do not, dire consequences will follow. Such consequences face the Church in the West. Rod Dreher has seen the jackals and the abject weakness of the church, just as in Ryle's day, and is calling us to repair the breaches in the wall before it is too late!

> I came to see the churches, including my own, as largely ineffective in combating the forces of cultural decline. Traditional, historic Christianity—whether Catholic, Protestant, or Eastern Orthodox— ought to be a powerful counterforce to the radical individualism and secularism of modernity. Even though conservative Christians were said to be fighting a culture war, with the exception of abortion and gay marriage issues, it was hard to see my people putting up much of a fight. We seemed content to be the chaplaincy to a consumer culture that was fast losing a sense of what it meant to be Christian.[4]

As a young Christian, I saw this pressure in 1974 to pull back from full-throttle Christianity in the village church I attended, in Tollerton near Nottingham. The vicar started faithfully preaching the gospel, outlining fallen human nature and the need to fight against the world, the flesh and the devil. Several parishioners were upset and asked him to stop because they were having sleepless nights; their consciences pricked by the Word of God. So, he stopped!

These pressures faced Timothy as Paul passed on the baton of ministry and leadership of the early church at a critical time. Saint Benedict wrote his short outline for those who wanted to keep their spiritual vitality in the storm of everything they had known crashing down around them. In a comparable way the storm facing the Western Church will test us to the limit as we face the collapse of Western Civilization. Tom Holland has shown, in his book, *Dominion*,[5] that a transcendent framework (Christianity) was essential for Western Civilization and now it is being widely repudiated (even though it is in the air we breathe). Life as we have known it will collapse since secular humanism cannot provide this framework. How should we prepare ourselves?

The importance of waking up to the seriousness of the situation

> Of Issachar, men who had understanding of the times to know what Israel ought to do (1 Chron 12:32).

Martyn Lloyd-Jones writes, 'There is nothing which shows our spiritual condition more clearly than our ability to comprehend the sign of the times.'[6] Carl R. Truman is one of the clearest and wisest voices today on understanding the signs of the times. In his book, *The Rise and Triumph of the Modern Self*,[7] he says we are complicit in bowing the knee to King Self. Instead, we need to bow the knee to

King Jesus in every aspect of our lives. When I got to the end of his book, I felt he must have been reading Philippians 1 and 2, when he gave the following three recommendations:

(1) THE CHURCH SHOULD UNDERSTAND WHAT IS GOING ON AND HOW BLEAK THE SITUATION IS FOR THE WESTERN CHURCH.

Philippians 2:1–5 says we are united with Christ; we have fellowship with the Spirit and with one another. We are to be like minded with Christ (v. 5). This is counter cultural. In Chapter 1:9–12 Paul's prayer for Christians at Philippi (facing great cultural pressure) is that 'love will abound more and more [Christian maturity] in knowledge and depth of insight so that you may be able to discern what is best and may be pure and blameless for the day of Christ'. How do we submit to the rule of King Jesus (2:10–12) in the context of today's culture? By growing in Christian maturity in the light of Christ's return, having the discernment of the seriousness of the impending collapse of Western Civilization and what that will mean.

(2) REFLECT LONG AND HARD ON THE CHURCH'S CORE BELIEFS AND PRACTICES.

'Stand firm' (Philippians 1:27; 4:1). To repeat the warning of Bishop J. C. Ryle, quoted earlier on page 36:

> The consequences of this widespread dislike to doctrine are very serious in the present day ... It produces what I must venture to call, if I may coin the phrase, a jellyfish Christianity in the churches—that is, a Christianity without bone, or muscle, or power

As already quoted but worth repeating, Truman writes,

'Christianity, as both Martin Luther and John Henry Newman knew, is dogmatic, doctrinal and assertive.'[8] He reflects that worldviews (we all have one) which capitulate on key doctrines collapse, while those who resist social pressure and keep their key beliefs thrive. We are seeing this in the Church of England where the churches that are teaching and upholding core beliefs on marriage are thriving and those who compromise are facing decline.

(3) THE CHURCH MUST BECOME A REAL COMMUNITY.

The church faces a challenge of authenticity, given the many serious scandals over sexual abuse and their later cover-ups, as well as widespread stories of bullying and coercion by some high-profile vicars and pastors. The culture already sees the church in its ethical teaching as oppressive and controlling, especially over gay marriage. Another problem is the many denominations and splits we see in the church. However, 'Communities,' argues Truman, 'are in flux across the world'. Globalization has seriously weakened the nation state (look at what happened to Liz Truss!) and the internet, while bringing many benefits, has undermined the concept of community (take for example the absurd phrase, 'Online Communities'). Truman writes that 'Our moral consciousness is very much shaped by our community.' He cites the LGBT community—while not supporting their aims—who have shown the strength of a community that helps its members in practical ways. The church must become a strong community that meets the needs of its members. This chimes in with what Rod Dreher says in his book, *The Benedict Option*.

The authority of the Bible is being attacked.

The sexual revolution since the 1960s has undermined the authority of the Bible and the Lordship of Christ. The church needs to recover its confidence in the Lord and his word and make sure we submit to Christ and turn from this world; it will mean suffering. The issue of the authority of God's Word is at the heart of what is going wrong in the Church of England. Its bishops need to repent and return to the Lord but, instead, they think they are hearing God's voice from the culture. They think they know more than the Bible writers and, particularly, that there was no knowledge of stable, long-term, loving, same-sex relationships in New Testament times. Former bishop, Tom Wright, has shown this not to be the case since there were such things with slaves and boys in the ancient world. The Bishop of Oxford has declared himself fully in favour of acceptance of same-sex blessing/marriage since the trajectory of the New Testament is freedom and equal worth for all. Others argue that Jesus says nothing about homosexuality. We will look at these points in future chapters.

> Meanwhile it is important to state that God made us in the image of God male and female (Genesis 1:27) and we find the foundation of marriage in Genesis 2 picked up and reaffirmed by Jesus in Matthew 19:5 as does the Apostle Paul in Ephesians 5:31. Any and all sexual activity which takes place outside of this context is treated as sinful, what Jesus calls 'sexual immorality' in Mark 7:21.[9]

Grace and truth

We also need to recognize that, because of the Fall described in Genesis 3, we are all born facing the wrath of God against sin and, while Romans 1 starts with wrath, the book itself is a theological tract to lead us to salvation by faith in Christ and his death for all sin, including homosexuality. The Bible's plot line involves Creation, Fall, Redemption and Renewal. Grace and truth go together in the Bible. John 1:17 says:

> For the law was given through Moses; grace and truth came through Jesus Christ.

We must remember how tough Jesus was with the Pharisees and the warm welcome he gave to all sinners to repent and experience transformation in Christ. We must give a loving welcome to everyone, no matter their background.

In my last year at my final parish, I was called by a man before the Sunday service to ask if we were welcoming of gay couples. He wanted to come to our church with his gay partner but was anxious about what sort of reaction they might face—they were on holiday from Ireland. I replied that we welcome everyone, since we are all sinners needing God's grace. I told him that we do stick to the Bible's teaching on human sexuality but that they would receive, like anyone else, a warm welcome. They came, enjoyed the service, and stayed for coffee afterwards. One of them remarked in conversation, 'We have found you so welcoming and wished we could find a church like yours where we live.'

What should our prayer be for the church in England?

In the next chapter, I will outline my own personal battle against false teaching in the Church of England and how the liberal drift of the Church of England has revealed itself by stages as the sexual revolution has impacted. While there are ministers and laity within the Church of England who have opposed these developments, the majority have slept while Rome burns. It is striking to recognize that what is happening in the Western Church and culture is as serious as the fall of Rome. The adage, 'Evil triumphs when good people do nothing', holds true in this as in other things. What should be our prayer at this vital time?

> Lord, help us to repent of 'jellyfish Christianity' and please send a spiritual revival to the Church in England. May we return to an authentic Christianity that builds your Church and reaches the nations for Christ. Help us to be faithful to you and your Word, even if it involves suffering and persecution. Amen.

NOTES

1 Dreher Rod, *The Benedict Option: A Strategy for Christians in a Post-Christian Nation*, (New York: Sentinel, 2017), p. 3.

2 www.thegospelcoalition.org/blogs/justin-taylor/5-quotes-that-luther-didnt-actually-say/

3 Ryle, J. C., 'The Importance of Dogma', 1900. www.gracegems.org/2017/10/Jellyfish Christianity.html

4 Dreher, Rod, *The Benedict Option: A Strategy for Christians in a Post-Christian Nation*, pp. 1–2.

5 Holland, Tom, *Dominion: The Making of the Western Mind*, (London: Little, Brown Book Group, 2019), pp. 517, 519.

6 Lloyd-Jones, D. Martyn, *Knowing the Times*, (Edinburgh: Banner of Truth, 1989), p. 17.

7 Trueman, Carl R., *The Rise and Triumph of the Modern Self*, pp. 402–404.

8 Ibid., p. 403.

9 Wood, Rob, 'What does the Bible teach about same-sex practice?' Updated: Nov 2020. https://truefreedomtrust.co.uk/what-does-bible-teach-about-same-sex-practice

4 Forty years of liberal drift in the Church of England

I t may appear that the mission to reach the UK for Christ is heading for disaster and failure, but God promises to sovereignly build his Church. However, God did not promise to build the Church of England, but Jesus did promise in Matthew 16:18, 'I will build my church, and the gates of hell shall not prevail against it.' We need to discern what God is doing in the Church in England, and understand what is happening in the culture, how we can survive the storm that is upon us, and preserve the orthodox faith in England, just as Benedict did after the fall of the Roman Empire. In this chapter, we will look at the instruction of Paul about false teachers in 2 Timothy and apply this to the last forty years of liberal drift in the Church of England, which led in February 2023 to the adoption of same-sex blessings.

II Timothy 2:14–26 has an exhortation to resist the false teachers.

Just before our last move from a vicarage when I retired at Easter 2022, it was the turn of the vicarage yard to have a clean-up. I used power washing to push back super-spreading, horrible green algae. As it builds up, it becomes very slippery and makes the yard dangerous; it spreads quickly and establishes itself. Sin is just like green algae. Paul is handing over to Timothy and encouraging him to fight the good fight against the false teachers: 'their talk will spread like gangrene' ... and they are 'upsetting the faith of some (vv. 17, 18)—like the horrible green algae in my former vicarage yard.

What is Paul's strategy?

Timothy is to outthink, out love and outshine the false teachers. The Christian faith has done this over the centuries, and this gives hope for the future. How does this work in practice? Paul reminds Timothy of the spiritual battle in 2:3: 'Share in suffering as a good soldier of Christ Jesus.' As we have already discovered, the great theme of 2 Timothy is faithfulness in the context of suffering. Timothy is to recognize the intense battle for truth, face up to the cost and play his part resolutely. As we have seen, persecution does not destroy God's church, but false teaching certainly will. We saw in Chapter 2, that we must contend for the faith once delivered and do it without striving in our own strength but trusting in the power of Christ within us through the Holy Spirit.

Verse 14: 'Remind them of these things.' Paul gives us things to embrace and things to avoid.

Things to embrace—be diligent in teaching the truth.

Verse 15: 'Do your best to present yourself to God as one approved, a worker who has no need to be ashamed, rightly handling the word of truth.'

'RIGHTLY HANDLING THE WORD OF TRUTH' ON THE SAME-SEX ISSUE?

It is tricky, isn't it? We have all seen this played out in UK politics with Tim Farron when he was leader of the Liberal Democrats and

Kate Forbes when she ran for leader of the SNP—both are committed Christians who were attacked by members of their own political parties for their Biblically orthodox views on homosexuality.

It is striking that, in Romans 14, Paul says we are to accept those whose faith is weak (we are all strong on some issues and weak on others) without judgement on disputable matters. However, Paul takes a vastly different approach in Romans 16:17 with warnings to keep away from false teachers. Issues vary in importance. Some things are secondary, while others are primary. False teaching comes in the primary category. We can agree to disagree with our brother or sister on secondary matters, but false teaching is too important to ignore since, as we have seen, while suffering does not destroy the church, false teaching always does.

In the previous chapter, I said that Jesus treated the Pharisees differently from the sinners and publicans. He denounced the Pharisees as blind guides and whitewashed tombs but had a lot of time and compassion for the sinners and publicans. In the parable of the Pharisee and the tax collector, it is the sinner who goes away from the temple justified before God, because he had repented from the heart (Luke 18:9–14). How would this apply to the gay issue? I would contend with a gay rights campaigner and pray for their salvation, while I would show patience and pastoral sensitivity to an ordinary gay couple, as I did when a gay couple came to our church service.

Things and people to avoid!

Avoid false teaching that spreads like gangrene:

> But avoid irreverent babble, for it will lead people into more and

more ungodliness, and their talk will spread like gangrene. Among
them are Hymenaeus and Philetus, who have swerved from the truth,
saying that the resurrection has already happened. They are
upsetting the faith of some (2 Timothy 2:16–18).

We are to avoid false teachers and recognize that their teaching is
destructive of people's faith and spreads rapidly like gangrene; so,
we need to take false teaching seriously. In 2 John, vv. 9–11, we read
these instructions about false teachers:

Everyone who goes on ahead and does not abide in the teaching of
Christ, does not have God. Whoever abides in the teaching has both
the Father and the Son. If anyone comes to you and does not bring
this teaching, do not receive him into your house or give him any
greeting, for whoever greets him takes part in his wicked works.

What do we make of this?

It must at least mean that we do not allow an erring bishop to preach
in our church or give financial support to his or her diocese, since
we are commanded not to take part in their wicked works. We should
not even welcome them into our home! To take such a strong
approach is against the grain of what we English call, 'being nice'.
Let us be clear: it is plainly wrong to give support to false teachers
and false teaching and we should act decisively. Parishes should cut
their parish shares (once they have covered costs of clergy) and give
the surplus towards helping poorer parishes and mission.

When did the rot start in the Church of England?

In 1984, the Bishop of Durham, David Jenkins, denied the bodily
resurrection of Christ. According to this senior bishop, Christ had

not been raised physically but spiritually and his body was still somewhere in Palestine! Orthodox Christians within the Church of England should have acted decisively, but there was little push back. If this central and key doctrine could be denied with impunity by a senior bishop, it opened the door for other areas like human sexuality and identity to be redefined. For me, it was a busy year getting married and, for the country, there was the miner's strike led by Arthur Scargill. Later, I would be vicar of the parish where Scargill grew up in Barnsley.

There have been numerous reports and some votes over the years in the General Synod of the Church of England about homosexuality, reflecting a steady liberal drift towards its acceptance in February 2023. Five years earlier, 'Living in Love and Faith' (LLF) was set up—a five-year engagement of the wide divergent views on human sexuality within the Church of England[1]—which significantly made no effort to look at the issue from a doctrinal and biblical point of view but was simply a presentation of the wide spectrum of views in the Church of England.

Moments of hope and encouragement

There have, however, been two moments of encouragement that stood out for orthodox Anglicans in England in the last forty years. The first was in 1987 when the General Synod passed the private member's motion—known as the Higton Motion after its evangelical sponsor, Rev. Tony Higton—which stated: 'Homosexual genital acts fall short of [God's] ideal and are to be met by a call to repentance and the exercise of compassion.'[2] However, this was a temporary victory and the slide continued in the Church of England.

Things were going little better in the Anglican Communion but, in1998, there was a significant statement made by the Lambeth Conference, reaffirmed since then by both GAFCON and the Global South. It was the last time there was serious theological debate and resolutions around the subject of human sexuality at that conference. Successive archbishops of Canterbury have since delayed, dithered, and refused to grasp the nettle and exercise effective discipline on erring liberal Provinces. Later, a device known as an 'Indaba', after an African approach to sort out tribal issues, was used to park the subject while things changed on the ground for the worse.

However, Lambeth 1998's *Resolution 1:10* was an incredibly significant marker for biblical orthodoxy on human sexuality among the Anglican Communion and still has the support of 75% of the Anglican Communion represented by GAFCON and the Global South. I was a vicar in Barnsley in 1998 when, just before the Lambeth Conference, the liberal bishop of Sheffield came for a chat. I asked him whether human sexuality would be an important subject at the conference. He thought for a while and then replied, 'Homosexuality will not figure at all at Lambeth.' How wrong he was!

1998 LAMBETH RESOLUTION 1:10 STATED:

- In view of the teaching of Scripture, upholds faithfulness in marriage between a man and a woman in lifelong union, and believes that abstinence is right for those who are not called to marriage.
- Recognises that there are among us persons who experience themselves as having a homosexual orientation. Many of

these are members of the church and are seeking the pastoral care, moral direction of the church, and God's transforming power for the living of their lives and the ordering of relationships. We commit ourselves to listen to the experience of homosexual persons and we wish to assure them that they are loved by God and that all baptised, believing, and faithful persons, regardless of sexual orientation, are full members of the Body of Christ.

• While rejecting homosexual practice as incompatible with Scripture, calls on all our people to minister pastorally and sensitively to all irrespective of sexual orientation and to condemn irrational fear of homosexuals, violence within marriage and any trivialisation and commercialisation of sex.

• Cannot advise the legitimising or blessing of same-sex unions nor ordaining those involved in same-gender unions.[3]

Facing the sack for sticking to the Bible

I was speaking to one of my church leaders in my last parish shortly before I retired, reflecting on my thirty-four years in the Church of England where trouble had followed me wherever I went. This started in my curacy in Cheadle, continued with my first vicar's job in Barnsley and then, happened again at Oldham. I said I was hoping to leave this last parish on a high note and not be thrown out for a change! 'Hmm,' said the church leader, 'there's time yet!'

My principled stand for truth almost cost me my job in 2002. However, in the end, the Bishop of Manchester recognized I was not a troublesome priest, but someone who followed his conscience no matter the cost. How did it get so serious?

An article I wrote for our parish magazine was passed to a local paper and then to the *Manchester Evening News* who ran this headline:

> A rebel vicar is set to remove his church from the Diocese of Manchester to find a more 'godly' bishop after a row over gay clergymen.
>
> The Rev. Steve Donald, vicar of Christ Church in Chadderton, says he is to take action after he claims the Bishop of Middleton, the Rt Rev. Michael Lewis, said he was willing to appoint homosexual ministers.
>
> The Rt Rev. Christopher Mayfield, Bishop of Manchester, said he was saddened by the claims. He said: 'This diocese has no intention of stepping outside the publicly agreed Church of England positions on faith and theology, ethics, and liturgy.'[4]

As I mentioned in Chapter 1, the Bishop of Middleton, an assistant bishop in Manchester Diocese, was due to lead a confirmation at Christ Church, Chadderton, but mentioned to me in private that he supported the ordination of homosexuals. I felt the Parochial Church Council should know and they supported me in refusing his ministry. At that point, we would have accepted another orthodox bishop from the diocese, but it went public and all four bishops closed ranks. Intense pressure was put on me to back down, which I refused to do on the grounds of conscience. I was facing the real possibility of being sacked for disobeying the bishop and inviting a retired missionary bishop to officiate at our confirmation instead.

Late in the day, as the confirmation drew near, the Bishop of Manchester graciously agreed to sign Lambeth 1:10, at my request, to clarify where he stood and bring this dispute between myself, the parish, and the diocese to an end. I, then, invited him to do our parish confirmation. I am sure he was genuine in his denial of a liberal drift in the Diocese of Manchester and the wider Church of England, but events have proved otherwise.

Years later in my last diocese, I used a freedom of information request to gain access to my confidential 'Blue File' on correspondence and reports concerning me during my time as a vicar. Gloria and I sat in the Bishop of Carlisle's office (since the document could not leave the premises) and read my confidential 'Blue file' and discovered that the Bishop of Manchester had discussed with his registrar whether to sack me or not! He concluded that I was not a troublesome priest but a man of conscience. What Christopher Mayfield, the Bishop of Manchester, did in signing Lambeth 1:10 and then taking our parish confirmation took courage and I hold him in profound respect. His decision to sign Lambeth 1:10 against the wishes of his fellow bishops in his diocese, reflected his commitment to the Canons and Articles of the Church of England.

CANON A5

Canon A5 (The Canons of the Church of England, 1969) states that the doctrine of the Church of England is grounded in the Holy Scriptures, and in such teachings of the ancient Fathers and Councils of the Church as are agreeable to the said Scriptures. In particular such doctrine is to be found in the Thirty-nine Articles of Religion, the Book of Common Prayer, and the Ordinal.

ARTICLE 20 OF THE THIRTY-NINE ARTICLES OF RELIGION.

> It is not lawful for the Church to ordain anything that is contrary to God's Word written.

After the consecration of Gene Robinson as the first gay bishop by the Episcopal Church in the United States, GAFCON was launched at Jerusalem in 2008. This was also a landmark meeting that produced the influential *Jerusalem Declaration*.

ARTICLE 8 OF THE *JERUSALEM DECLARATION* DEALS WITH HUMAN SEXUALITY.

> We acknowledge God's creation of humankind as male and female and the unchangeable standard of Christian marriage between one man and one woman as the proper place for sexual intimacy and the basis of the family. We repent of our failures to maintain this standard and call for a renewed commitment to lifelong fidelity in marriage and abstinence for those who are not married.[5]

In its closing comments it said:

> The meeting in Jerusalem this week was called in a sense of urgency that a false gospel has so paralysed the Anglican Communion that this crisis must be addressed. The chief threat of this dispute involves the compromising of the integrity of the church's worldwide mission. The primary reason we have come to Jerusalem and issued this declaration is to free our churches to give clear and certain witness to Jesus Christ.[6]

Since 2008, GAFCON has given clear direction to confessing Anglicans unhappy about the liberal direction of the Anglican

Communion, and the *Jerusalem Declaration* has provided a theological framework for dealing with the crisis. The fourth meeting in April 2023 in Kigali, Rwanda, will mark another landmark conference in setting a direction for mission and discipleship and the call for a radical reset of the Anglican Communion structures with the Archbishop of Canterbury no longer giving leadership as 'first among equals'. This is because of his support for same-sex blessings. As mentioned in Chapter 1, GAFCON and the Global South share the same theology and vision for the way ahead but differ on strategy.

Eventually both groups will help reset the Anglican Communion based on Scripture, reason, and tradition.

Ecumenism is the Handmaiden of Progressive Liberalism.

In 2005, I moved to an evangelical diocese which has now become ecumenical and revisionist under the same bishop who has consistently argued for traditional marriage yet voted in favour of same-sex blessings!

> On Sunday, 27 November 2011, church leaders from the Methodist, United Reformed and Anglican Churches in Cumbria signed an ecumenical *Declaration of Intent* to work together in the first Ecumenical County. The Bishop of Carlisle said, to a meeting of concerned evangelical clergy, that the covenant would be dissolved if one of the denominations accepted same-sex blessings/marriage.[7]

In 2021, the Methodist church accepted same-sex marriage but the covenant in Cumbria is still in existence![8]

In spite of being very public about his support for traditional marriage, the Bishop of Carlisle, as already stated, voted in favour of same-sex blessings at the General Synod in February 2023 and this is on public record.[9] (In making statements about other ministers in the Church of England, I have generally limited my comments to their public statements that can be found on the internet. In calling or inferring that some of them are 'false teachers', 'wolves in sheep's clothing' and so on, I am confining myself to the example of Scripture in both Old and New Testaments and the example of Jesus himself! Given the Bible's warning that false teachers and their teaching leads to the destruction of the church this is clearly warranted and reasonable.)

Ecumenism without a confessional commitment to biblical truth is the handmaiden of progressive liberalism. The decision of the Bishop of Carlisle to support traditional marriage yet vote for same-sex blessings would be inconceivable except for the recognition that ecumenism waters down doctrinal distinctives and leaves what Bishop J. C. Ryle called 'jellyfish Christianity'.

What explains the slow liberal drift in the Church of England culminating in the acceptance of same-sex blessings in February 2023? False teaching is one explanation, but false teachers can be resisted and discipline exerted so their teaching does not spread like gangrene and endanger the health of the church. But the Church of England and the Anglican Communion lack effective means of discipline, one of the essential marks of a healthy church according to the Reformation. The other explanation of this spiritual decline over the last forty years must be due, in some part, to orthodox believers in the Church of England, both clergy and laity, who have lost their courage to suffer for the gospel by being willing to stand up and stand out for Christ and his Word. The Lord Jesus uttered a solemn warning in Mark 8:38, that we must take seriously in the light of his Lordship and promised return to judge:

> For whoever is ashamed of me and of my words in this adulterous and sinful generation, of him will the Son of Man also be ashamed when he comes in the glory of his Father with the holy angels.

Notice how the Lord connects being 'ashamed of me and my words'. To be ashamed of the clear teaching of Scripture is to be ashamed of Christ himself! In the next chapter, we will look at the powerful cultural forces behind the sexual revolution in the Church of England over the last forty years. If the ark stands for the confessing church, then the sea stands for the world. When the sea gets in the ark it sinks. We are to be in the world but not of it, since we have a great hope of salvation and a new world to look forward to in heaven.

What sort of sea are we facing?

Certainly, much stormier waves than we have already faced. Are we facing a George Orwell's *1984* dystopian culture—a soft totalitarianism that rules by fear—or a culture more akin to Aldous Huxley's *Brave New World*, where, in Chapter 17 of the book, the world controller wants the dissident to join them and offers him 'Christianity without tears'. This has always been a seductive ploy playing to a hedonistic culture.

Whatever the nature of the storm coming, the church needs to heed the warnings from those who, like the men of Issachar, understood the times and knew what to do (1 Chronicles 12:32).

Both Rod Dreher and Carl Truman would agree on the seriousness of the situation, the essential need to hold fast to our doctrines and core beliefs, and the urgency to build arks of community to weather the storm that is certainly coming. In the next chapter, 2 Timothy 3 will help us to recognize that evil is widespread, see sin for what it is and respond wisely—to positively fill our minds with the truth of Jesus Christ. These things will help us survive and even thrive in the storm.

NOTES

1 See Glossary of terms on page 126.
2 www.thinkinganglicans.org.uk/uploads/GS%20Misc%20843a.pdf
3 https://www.churchsociety.org/wp-content/uploads/2021/05/lambeth_1_10.pdf
4 www.manchestereveningnews.co.uk/news/greater-manchester-news/vicar-to-break-away-in-gay-1187539
5 *The Jerusalem Declaration* 2008, Article 8. www.gafcon.org/about/jerusalem-declaration.
6 *The Jerusalem Statement*, www.gafcon.org/about/jerusalem-statement
7 www.methodist.org.uk/about-us/news/latest-news/all-news/cumbria-becomes-first-ecumenical-county-in-england/
8 www.bbc.co.uk/news/uk-england-57658161
9 https://premierchristian.news/en/news/article/how-church-of-england-bishops-voted-same-sex-blessings-during-general-synod

5 Times of difficulty will arise

Tom Holland's book, *Dominion*, demonstrates that liberal Western Culture is dependent on the Christian faith, since it is in the air we breathe. Western Society needs a transcendent faith; secular humanism cannot hold it together. Titus 1:1 (NIV) states: *The truth that leads to godliness.* No truth, no godliness! Spartan and Roman culture were brutal. Babies who did not have certain physical characteristics were left on the hillside by their parents to die. Holland concludes that it was the advent of Christianity that brought a value to everyone and care for the weak. Without Christian doctrine underpinning Western Culture, it will fall. Nietzsche,[1] a profoundly influential German philosopher, announced the 'death of God', but the shadows of the corpse, he explained (in his famous parable), represented millions who still cling to belief in God.[2]

Physical persecution of the Church may begin in the UK as breakdown of order leads the government and the institution of the Church of England to become more restrictive and controlling. This happened during the Covid-19 pandemic when the Church of England, operating as a zealous extension of the state, imposed more restrictions than the state required, even closing churches for prayer and to vicars. If there was ever a need for the church to open its doors it was during the pandemic, yet churches were instructed to close and harsh measures applied to anyone who showed any opposition.

Why would the state and institution of the church persecute confessional Christians on the issue of homosexuality? 'Every sensible man,' Voltaire wrote, 'every honourable man, must hold the Christian sect in horror.'[3] Why would the present state and institution of the church hold the Christian sect in horror? Because orthodox Christians, following the plain teaching of the Bible, continue to insist that homosexual acts are sinful, and the culture and the progressive institutional church sees such attitudes as toxic and oppressive.

Rather than acknowledge that his ethical principles might owe anything to Christianity, (writes Holland of Voltaire) he preferred to derive them from a range of other sources—not just classical literature, but Chinese philosophy and his own powers of reason. Yet Voltaire, in his concern for the weak and oppressed, was marked more enduringly by the stamp of biblical ethics than he cared to admit. His defiance of the Christian God, in a paradox that was certainly not unique to him, drew on motivations that were, in part at least, recognisably Christian.[4]

The same paradox applies today to both state and state-church attitudes. They fail to see that confessional Christianity underpins a caring society where everyone (including LGBTQ+ community) has value as people made in the image of God and the weak are protected, since it is, 'the truth that leads to godliness'. No Christian doctrinal underpinning of society, no godliness. That is not to say that you can only be moral if you are a Christian. It is rather to say that Christianity had a profound impact for good on Western Civilization and now, that good is under threat. The Christian faith is seen as toxic and immoral by a growing number of people.

Freedom of speech underpinned by Christian tolerance is also being eroded and rolled back.

Under the current domination of 'woke' ideology, anyone who takes an alternative view is vilified, deplatformed and seen as the enemy of progress. It is only a short step away from persecuting the 'guilty'. The state shows little interest in resisting the 'woke' agenda and the Archbishop of Canterbury's position (giving a particular political steer rather than a spiritual one) is to support the progressive liberal agenda. *The New Statesman* recently (June 8th, 2023) brought out a list of the top fifty left-wing people who influence society and Justin Welby came in at number twenty-seven![5]

There would appear to be no circumstances where the archbishop himself would suffer physical persecution for his faith but every possibility of his leading harsh measures against those who hold to the Bible on homosexuality. This was suggested by the archbishop's response to a demonstration outside Lambeth Palace following the February 2023 General Synod Vote when, under pressure from gay activists, the archbishop promised to 'deal with those priests' who offer to pray with those struggling with same-sex desires wanting to adhere to celibacy.[6]

2 Timothy 3:1–9

Verse 1 in this passage predicts that 'In the last days there will come times of difficulty.' (Hence the title of this chapter.) The 'last days' began when Christ appeared on earth. We would expect an increase in evil since, the reason the Son of God appeared was to destroy the works of the devil (1 John 3:8). The second letter to

Timothy 3:2–5 paints a grim picture of fallen human nature in rebellion against God:

> For people will be lovers of self, lovers of money, proud, arrogant, abusive, disobedient to their parents, ungrateful, unholy, heartless, unappeasable, slanderous, without self-control, brutal, not loving good, treacherous, reckless, swollen with conceit, lovers of pleasure rather than lovers of God, having the appearance of godliness, but denying its power.

'For people will be lovers of self,' accurately describes our present culture. This section in 2 Timothy describes in lurid detail what is known as the doctrine of original sin—an idea difficult for human beings to accept, even Christians. C. S. Lewis wrote:

> For a long time, I used to think this a silly, straw-splitting distinction: how could you hate what a man did and not hate the man? But years later it occurred to me that there was one man to whom I had been doing this all my life—namely myself... In fact, the very reason why I hated the things was that I loved the man. Just because I loved myself, I was sorry to find that I was the sort of man who did those things... (I was) hoping, if it is in any way possible, that somehow, sometime, somewhere, he can be cured and made human again.[7]

We find that transformative promise in the gospel of Christ and that is the sort of spiritual leadership we should be getting from the Archbishop of Canterbury. But he has abdicated spiritual leadership and instead taken up a political agenda for both church and state.

By including a typical vice list (2 Timothy 3: 2–5), Paul connects the defections of the false teachers with the general increase of evil everywhere, which is evidence that the final days have arrived. By connecting them to the subversion of weak women (vv. 6–7) and by comparing them to the Egyptian magicians who opposed Moses (vv. 8–9), Paul shows that the false teachers are just religious charlatans, comparable to the sorcerers and charlatans the ancient world was familiar with. (For charlatans today, read about 'American TV evangelists' or 'most of the House of Bishops in the Church of England!')

The second letter to Timothy 3:13 warns, 'Evildoers and impostors will go on from bad to worse, deceiving and being deceived.'

The Bible says things will get worse before they get better. We are a people of the cross. Our faith will be severely tested. This section of 2 Timothy tells us three things:

1) EXPECT EVIL TO BE WIDESPREAD (2 TIMOTHY 3:1–2).

This is an accurate picture of society without God: corrupt, wicked, and getting more wicked by the day—just what the Bible says will happen. Sin is simply ignoring God in the world he has made, but that sin separates us not only from God but also from one another.

2) SEE SIN FOR WHAT IT IS SO YOU CAN RESPOND WISELY (2 TIMOTHY 3:2–7).

We can be so naïve. Jesus instructed us to be 'wise as serpents and innocent as doves' (Matthew 10:16). What are the biggest problems facing society today? Surely *addiction* must be number one—addiction to drugs, sex, and computers/mobile phones. What should the church be doing? Changing destructive habits to life enhancing ones by the application of gospel medicine.

3) FILL YOUR MIND WITH THE TRUTH OF JESUS CHRIST (2 TIM 3:8–9).

Do the opposite of these men, described in these verses, who oppose the truth! Do all you can to get a Christian mind. (For example: meditate on Romans 12:2: 'Do not be conformed to this world, but be transformed by the renewal of your mind, that by testing you may discern what is the will of God, what is good and acceptable and perfect.') How do we turn destructive habits into life-enhancing ones? By developing a Christian mind since as we think, so we live. For this we need the truth and as the Lord Jesus said, 'The truth will set you free' (John 8:32).

If the confessing church is the ark and the world is the sea, then if the water gets into the ark it sinks! In this book, my contention has been that physical persecution will not destroy the church, as demonstrated by Paul in 2 Timothy, and that false teaching always will destroy a church and must therefore be resisted. But how are we to identify false teachers? Two things will identify the faithful teacher: adherence to sound doctrine from the Scriptures and holy living. The absence of these shows us who are the false teachers in the church—those whom Jesus and Paul call 'ferocious wolves' among the sheep.

When it comes to spotting false teachers, who are we to keep away from? (Romans 16:17). What are we to use to discern whether they are 'sheep' or 'wolves in sheep's clothing?' Firstly, compare what they teach with the Scriptures. If their teaching is contrary to Scripture keep away from them. Secondly, consider the fruit of their lives. Jesus said in Mathew 7:15–16:

> Beware of false prophets, who come to you in sheep's clothing but

inwardly are ravenous wolves. You will recognize them by their fruits.

Bishop J. C. Ryle in his book, *Expository Thoughts on the Gospels*, page 46 writes on these verses:

> Teaching must be weighed in the balance of Holy Scripture. [Clergymen] are to be followed and believed, so long as their doctrine agrees with the Bible, but not a minute longer. We are to try them by their 'fruits'.'[8]

Watch out for false prophets.

Since the Archbishop of Canterbury and the House of Bishops have voted for same-sex blessings, they have become false teachers who must be avoided and resisted. Meanwhile, the orthodox-confessing church needs to acknowledge the seriousness of the cultural storm that is coming, hold firmly to its doctrinal credal beliefs and build community. Build an ark to ride out the storm.

In the next chapter we will see the critical need to discern competing worldviews so that we can embrace the one built on Scripture, Reason and Tradition and turn away from the one built on human reason which rejects the authority of Scripture. We need to build an ark to survive the storm that is upon us.

NOTES

1 Friedrich Wilhelm Nietzsche (October 15, 1844 – August 25, 1900) was a profoundly influential German philosopher, psychologist, and classical philologist. Particularly aggressive, he was a severe critic of Christian morality... Although his work was distorted

and thus identified with Philosophical Romanticism, Nihilism, Anti-semitism, and even Nazism, he himself vociferously denied such tendencies in his work, so much as to directly opposing them. In philosophy and literature, he is often identified as an inspiration for existentialism and postmodernism. https://www.theopedia.com/friedrich-nietzsche

2 https://en.wikisource.org/wiki/Page:Complete_works_of_Nietzsche_vol_10.djvu/163

3 www.newstatesman.com/politics/religion/2016/09/tom-holland-why-i-was-wrong-about-christianity

4 Ibid.

5 https://anglican.ink/2023/06/08/the-new-statesmans-left-power-list/

6 www.newstatesman.com/politics/religion/2016/09/tom-holland-why-i-was-wrong-about-christianity

7 Lewis, C. S., *Mere Christianity*, (London: Harper Collins, 1952), page 134.

8 Ryle, J. C., *Expository Thoughts on the Gospels: Matthew*, (Welwyn, Herts: Evangelical Press, 1985), p. 46.

6 Discerning truth and error

How do we know whether someone is a faithful minister 'rightly handling the word of truth' (2 Timothy 2:15), or a false teacher, 'deceiving and being deceived'? (2 Timothy 3:13). Our first instinct should be to open our Bibles and ask, 'What does the Scripture say?' (Romans 4:3). The Bible is a reliable and sufficient Word that enables us to live a life of godliness and, as the Reformers taught, it is perspicuous—which means it is clear and understandable. John Foxe, in his book, *Foxe's Book of Martyrs*, attributes the following famous saying to William Tyndale: 'If God spare my life, ere many years I will cause a boy who drives the plough to know more of the Scriptures than you do.' (Tyndale was in a discussion with a clergyman.)[1]

> Tyndale was a 16th-century priest and scholar who translated the Bible into an early form of 'modern' English. Although some English translations had been previously made, Tyndale's was the first to take advantage of the new medium of print, which allowed for its wide distribution. Forbidden to work in England, Tyndale translated and printed in English the New Testament and half the Old Testament between 1525 and 1535 in Germany and the Low Countries. He worked from the Greek and Hebrew original texts when knowledge of those languages in England was rare.[2]

Remarkably, we owe about two-thirds of our modern Bibles to Tyndale's work, and we rely on accurate translations unless we read the original languages! Tyndale was a faithful and courageous minister who was martyred for his insistence that the Bible ought to be in the language of the common people.

Of course, there are difficult parts of the Bible to interpret, but another principle the Reformers taught was to compare the clear with the difficult passages that deal with the same subject. When it comes to the Bible's teaching on human sexuality, it is noticeably clear and has been accepted by the church for two thousand years. The Church of England, in its formularies, looks to the Scriptures for its doctrines. We either sit under the Scriptures or set ourselves above them. When we listen to teaching, we should be like the noble Bereans in Acts 17:11 who 'received the word with all eagerness, examining the Scriptures daily to see if these things were so'.

Style over substance

If a sermon was entertaining and enjoyable it can sometimes be rated as a good sermon, even though the content was shallow or even in error. If it is no more than ten minutes in length it gets extra brownie points! However, good sermons should be Christ centred, biblically accurate, gripping, and of sound content and appropriate length. There is nothing worse than a dull vicar but, as the saying goes, 'Sermonettes, produce Christianettes.'

Another problem can be the personality of the preacher. False teachers can often be nice guys. For example, Arius, a theologian who lived AD 256–336, was charismatic and popular but wrong, while Athanasius was blunt but right about the issue of the nature of Christ! Aruis taught that the Son of God was not eternal, and his views were declared to be heretical at the Council of Nicaea, from which we get the Nicene Creed.

In this chapter, we will consider the interchange between the Bishop of Oxford, Steven Croft, and a member of his clergy, Vaughan Roberts, Rector of St Ebbs Oxford. Bishop Steven argues for the acceptance of same-sex blessings and gay marriage, while Vaughan Roberts believes his bishop's proposals are against Scripture, reason, and tradition. How do we know which of these prominent ministers are reflecting the will of God? We get the criteria from 2 Timothy 3:10–17, where Paul deals with this question:

> You, however, have followed my teaching, my conduct, my aim in life, my faith, my patience, my love, my steadfastness, my persecutions and sufferings that happened to me at Antioch, at Iconium, and at Lystra—which persecutions I endured; yet from them all the Lord rescued me. Indeed, all who desire to live a godly life in Christ Jesus will be persecuted, while evil people will go on from bad to worse, deceiving and being deceived. But as for you, continue in what you have learned and have firmly believed, knowing from whom you learned it and how from childhood you have been acquainted with the sacred writings, which are able to make you wise for salvation through faith in Christ Jesus. All Scripture is breathed out by God and profitable for teaching, for reproof, for correction, and for training in righteousness, that the man of God may be competent, equipped for every good work.

The apostle Paul gives two criteria for assessing someone's teaching, which we saw earlier in the quote from Bishop J. C. Ryle. Firstly, Paul states that the true teacher's life will be holy and secondly, he will be faithful in his preaching to what the Scriptures say about itself, namely that 'All Scripture is breathed out by God and profitable for teaching, for reproof, for correction, and for training in righteousness' (verse 16). The plenary inspiration of Scripture means every part of it is profitable for study and application for life and godliness. Paul links both lip and life together: 'You, however, have followed my teaching, my conduct' (v. 10). Paul links faithfulness in teaching the Scriptures accurately with conduct that is holy, i.e., pleasing to God. He also indicates that suffering will be part of faithfulness to the gospel, just as it was for Paul (v. 11) and will be for every faithful believer (v. 12).

How do we discern truth and error: a case in point

What about these two men who stand either side of the controversy regarding same-sex blessings and gay marriage? I know Vaughan Roberts as a very able teacher and godly man. I have read two of his books on human sexuality and found them helpful. Vaughan, in my view, rightly handles the word of God (2 Timothy 2:15). He has a reputation for transparency and is beyond reproach in his personal conduct. He has been open about being same sex attracted but maintains a celibate life.

The way in which we can assess whether someone is a faithful or false teacher is to compare what they say with the plain teaching of the Bible. Paul says, in 2 Timothy 3:13: 'Evil people and impostors will go on from bad to worse, deceiving and being deceived.' Paul elsewhere in the letter is not afraid to name false teachers (1:15; 2:17; 4:10). This seems very harsh to our modern ears but, if someone like Bishop Steven is teaching error, it is a serious matter potentially sending people to hell, since we are told in 1 Corinthians 6 that 'the unrighteous will not inherit the Kingdom of God,' and includes 'men who practice homosexuality' (v. 9).

Rightly handle the word of truth

Let us compare Bishop Steven's teaching with the Scriptures and the teaching of the church through the ages. A wise lecturer at my theological college said:

> If you come up with a new interpretation of the Bible that no one else has seen in the history of the church be extremely cautious. You may have discovered something new but be incredibly careful to assess it by Scripture, Tradition and Reason.

How does Bishop Steven's essay advocating same-sex blessings and gay marriage look when we apply these three criteria? I will seek to represent Bishop Steven accurately (within the limitations of just a chapter) and then give my response, including a link to Vaughan Roberts' booklet and some of the points he makes.

Sound exegesis begins with expounding the Bible and having gone (as it were in our minds) to Corinth or Jerusalem (depending on what part of Scripture we are expounding) faithful preachers seek to bring its timeless message to the 21st century—in my case to the UK where I live. Martyn Lloyd-Jones, a prominent Free Church leader of the 1960s gave his view of Bishop Ryle's handling of the Bible in his introduction to a new printing of Ryle's book, *Holiness*:

> The characteristics of Bishop Ryle's method and style are obvious. He is pre-eminently and always scriptural and expository. He never starts with a theory into which he tries to fit various Scriptures. He always starts with the Word and expounds it. It is exposition at its very best and highest. It is always clear and logical and invariably leads to a clear enunciation of doctrine.[3]

We have here an extremely helpful description of how to rightly handle the word of truth. Lloyd-Jones says Ryle's method and style is 'pre-eminently and always scriptural and expository... It is always clear and logical and invariably leads to a clear enunciation of doctrine.' This is how we should discern what the Bible says on human sexuality by starting with an exposition of the relevant texts, not just those that prohibit homosexuality but also the Bible's teaching on the broad sweep of Scripture, the incredibly positive instruction on marriage from Genesis to Revelation, including the affirmation of biblical marriage by Jesus in Matthew 19 and his and Paul's high view of singleness. This can then lead to a clear enunciation of doctrine. We must start with the Bible rather than start with a theory and work towards it. To start with a theory and then look to the Bible is not a helpful theological method because you will get the answer you seek rather than what the Bible actually says. Taking Ryle's positive example, Lloyd-Jones gives a warning of what to avoid. 'He [Ryle] never starts with a theory into which he tries to fit various Scriptures.' This is exactly the mistake Bishop Steven makes in his essay.

Bishop Steven's theory

Bishop Steven begins with 'The testimony of the whole of Scripture to human equality and worth.'[4] This is taught in the Bible and is something that few would question but should we not begin with what the Bible says about human sexuality made in the image of God and representing the wonderful covenant between God and his Church at the start? Framing the enquiry by beginning with human equality in this way excludes consideration of the holiness of God and his wrath against sin and twists the Scripture to fit what Bishop Steven wants to say. God is a God of grace and mercy, but also a God of judgement. His mercy does triumph over judgement but only for those who repent and believe the gospel. All of us are sinners needing the gospel because 'All have sinned and fall short of the glory of God' (Romans 3:23). Bishop Steven's view that pastoral needs trump Scriptural truth is exposed when he writes:

> As I listen to the stories and experiences of LGBTQ+ people, all of my pastoral instincts point to finding a way of interpreting the Scriptures that allows for greater love and support, tolerance and the blessing of their partnerships, even where this interpretation seems, at first sight, to be in conflict with some of the obvious interpretations of key biblical passages.[5]

Principles of interpretation

Professor John Lennox makes a general point while looking at the text of Genesis 1 and 2, which is helpful in looking at Bishop Steven's handling of Scripture:

> [There] is an important exegetical principle, which is that we should pay careful attention to what the text says before trying to decide what it means ... If we believe in the inspiration of Scripture, we must take the text seriously, because it is Scripture that is inspired and not our particular understanding of it.[6]

It seems to me that Bishop Steven ignores this key exegetical principle. He does not look at a text as if he has not seen it before, asking for illumination. Instead, he makes his pastoral priority override the plain teaching of Scripture to find 'a way of interpreting the Scriptures that allows' the church to accept same-sex blessings and marriage. This is not sound exegesis.

Vaughan Robert's response

Vaughan Roberts gives an excellent response to Bishop Steven's essay and I heartily commend it. He helpfully remarks that he thinks this is not about the interpretation of Scripture but its authority. This is a crucial point which links with his emphasis that we need to consider roots as well as fruits. Vaughan suggests there are two gospels to choose from which are rooted in two opposing world views:

> Describing how, especially for a younger generation, the church's traditional position on sexuality is seen to fall short of their deeply felt standards of justice and fairness, he (Bishop Steven) comments: 'we are seen to inhabit a different moral universe.' He is right about that, but he fails to engage with the reality that the difference goes way beyond contrasting approaches to one issue alone but is the result of a completely different mindset about the whole of life, which is manifest in the sexual revolution of the last few decades. It is important to recognise both the roots of that revolution, as well as its fruits. Beginning with roots, the difference between the moral instincts of contemporary society and the traditional teaching of the church flows from two different worldviews, both of which could be called gospels, because each claim to present good news which offers an alternative path to freedom and fulfilment.[7]

This shows that what is at stake is not simply a biblical view of human sexuality, but the biblical gospel itself.

Bishop Steven uses analogies rather than first principles that enable him to sidestep the clear teaching of the bible that homosexuality is sinful:

> Many Christians take the inherited position because they attempt to work from first principles: What does the Bible say we should do (or what has the church traditionally taught)? In this view, the first principles are drawn from the biblical prohibitions, all active same-sex relationships are seen as wrong and the pastoral practice of the church should therefore continue to reflect this view. But suppose we begin not with these first principles but from analogies. What is this permanent, faithful, stable, long-term partnership between people of the same sex most like? Does it resemble promiscuous and immoral behaviour? Or does it resemble much more closely something that is very like a Christian understanding of marriage? I would argue, very much the latter. On the grounds of this analogy, the church should therefore conform its pastoral practice to this new understanding.[8]

One of Bishop Steven's main arguments for changing our doctrine of human sexuality is that the mission of the church is impaired because there is a disconnect between church and society on the issue of homosexuality. The church must change its doctrine so it can serve the whole of society. It is striking that what he says is the exact opposite of what the *Jerusalem Declaration* says, which I quoted earlier in Chapter 4.

The *Jerusalem Declaration*'s closing comments state:

> The meeting in Jerusalem this week was called in a sense of urgency that a false gospel has so paralysed the Anglican Communion that this crisis must be addressed. The chief threat of this dispute involves the compromising of the integrity of the church's worldwide mission.

The primary reason we have come to Jerusalem and issued this declaration is to free our churches to give clear and certain witness to Jesus Christ.[9]

This illustrates the point made earlier in my quotation from Vaughan Roberts:

Beginning with roots, the difference between the moral instincts of contemporary society and the traditional teaching of the church flows from two different worldviews, both of which could be called gospels, because each claims to present good news which offers an alternative path to freedom and fulfilment.[10]

The church, as the Jerusalem Declaration states, is called to be counter-cultural, just as the early church was confronted by a godless society which, through faithful Christian witness and suffering, was transformed by the gospel, getting rid of infanticide and gladiatorial games. Tom Holland has shown that it was Christianity that brought ideas of the worth of every single person made in the image of God and care for the vulnerable and weak, that have formed the bedrock of Western Civilization. LGBTQ+ people are in the category of a minority who have been subject to discrimination and prejudice, sometimes at the hands of conservative Christians. For that we must say sorry and do all we can to treat everyone with respect as human beings made in the image of God.

We should also pray for same sex attracted Christians who want to live a celibate life, following the traditional teaching on marriage and singleness. This is a tough road, not made easier by being told by bishops that their sacrifice and struggle is not necessary.

Fortunately, there are excellent support groups called *Living Out and True Freedom Trust*, which Bishop Steven did not mention in his essay, but which Vaughan commends.

I am limited to a chapter on this subject and would suggest you read both Bishop Steven's essay and Vaughan Roberts' response. One of the few points of common ground (amid significant and deep disagreement) was the point raised by Bishop Steven and Vaughan about the massive change in Western Culture. Vaughan says:

> There is no doubt that the cultural changes over the last few decades in relation to sexuality have resulted in significant dislocation between church and society. Whereas not long ago a traditional Christian approach to sexuality was widely affirmed, even if it was less commonly practised, it is now often regarded as harmful and even immoral. Those who seek to uphold orthodoxy in these matters in the church are regarded as heretics in the world, in resisting values and beliefs that, it is assumed by many, should be upheld by all right-thinking people.
>
> Bishop Steven is certainly right in recognizing the missional challenge caused by these cultural shifts, but there is, of course, nothing new in the church experiencing such dissonance within and hostility from its surrounding culture. In fact, the Lord Jesus told his disciples to expect no less: 'You do not belong to the world, but I have chosen you out of the world. That is why the world hates you' (John 15:19). In the history of the global Church down the ages a gap between it and the society it inhabits has been normal. In such circumstances, the question which arises is whether that gap can and should be reduced by wise cultural adaptation for the sake of mission ('To the Jews I became like a Jew, to win the Jews', 1 Corinthians 9:20), or whether such changes should be resisted out of faithfulness to the apostolic faith.[11]

False teaching and false teachers must be resisted

I think the answer to Vaughan's question is now obvious as we have considered the roots as well as the fruit of this new way of looking at the Bible. Such changes are embraced because of a lack of confidence and belief in the authority of Scripture, rather than a convincing new interpretation or 'cultural adaption for the sake of mission', and such changes to doctrine should be 'resisted out of faithfulness to the Apostolic faith'. In the next chapter, we will look at the storm that is coming with the collapse of Western Culture, which thinkers like Rod Dreher say will be as serious as the fall of the Roman Empire. We will seek to trace the origins of this massive cultural shift that both Bishop Steven and Vaughan Roberts agreed upon, which go back hundreds of years and attempt to plot its future progress.

NOTES

1 Foxe, John, *Actes and Monuments of These Latter and Perilous Dayes*, (London: John Day, 1563), p. 570.

2 www.theopedia.com/william-tyndale

3 Lloyd-Jones, D. M., cited in: Ryle, J. C., *Holiness*, Introduction. https://www.apuritansmind.com/wp-content/uploads/FREEEBOOKS/Holiness-J.C.Ryle.pdf

4 Croft, Steven, Bishop of Oxford, *Together in Love and Faith: Personal Reflections and next Steps for the Church*, (Oxford: Diocese of Oxford, 2022), p. 25. https://d3hgrlq6yacptf.cloudfront.net/61f2fd86f0ee5/content/pages/documents/together-in-love-and-faith.pdf

5 Ibid., pp. 27–28.

6 Lennox, Professor John, *Seven Days that Divide the World*, (Grand Rapids, Michigan: Zondervan, 2011), loc 59.

7 Roberts, Vaughan, *Together in Love and Faith? A Response to the Bishop of Oxford*, (London: Latimer Press, 2022), pp. 14–15. A free download is available on https://www.latimertrust.org/

8 Croft, Steven, Bishop of Oxford, *Together in Love and Faith: Personal Reflections and next Steps for the Church*, p. 41.

9 *The Jerusalem Statement*, 2008. www.gafcon.org/about/jerusalem-statement. Sourced: 19/07/24

10 Roberts, Vaughan, *Together in Love and Faith? A Response to the Bishop of Oxford*, pp. 14–15.

11 Roberts, Vaughan, *Together in Love and Faith? A Response to the Bishop of Oxford*, pp. 13–14.

7 A cultural revolution is upon us

It has taken a long time to arrive at this cultural breaking point, the imminent collapse of Western Civilization that could be as serious as the fall of the Roman Empire. Why is this happening? The cultural tectonic plates have been moving for a while, but Rod Dreher believes that the mass savagery of World War I dealt a 'mortal blow to what remained of Christendom'. He quotes sociologist, Zygmunt Bauman, about what he sees as the move from '"solid modernity"'—a period of social change that was still fairly predictable and manageable—to "liquid modernity", our present condition, in which change is so rapid that no social institutions have time to solidify.'[1]

Without social institutions, Western Culture will eventually collapse. A prominent feature in this liquid modernity is *Gender Ideology*.

What is gender ideology and where did it come from?
In this chapter, we will examine the powerful ideas which are sweeping away the stability and the way of life of the post-war years and trace their origins. These ideas are known by different terms such as Cultural Marxism, Critical Theory or Neo Marxism. Antonio Gramsci (1860–1937), a neo-Marxist and founding member of the Italian Communist party, is credited with being a sort of founding father to these ideas, but they have their roots in several thinkers who promoted the idea of the central importance of the human self

many years before, including Rousseaux (the psychological self), Freud (the sexual self) and Marx (the political self). Gramsci was critical of Soviet Communism under Stalin and was frustrated there were no further Marxist revolutions between the world wars; he believed it was because workers had bought into the worldview of the middle classes. It required an alternative worldview, he argued, that highlighted conflict between the oppressed and the oppressors.

Working with the Frankfurt School, Gramsci and others produced concepts such as 'intersectionality', which divides society into grievance groups. Status is based on a group identity and conflict between oppressed and oppressors. In this worldview, identity conflict replaces the class conflict of classical Marxism. Critical theory then becomes an umbrella group under which all other sub worldviews like LGBTQ+, feminism, race issues and even ecology can find a home. The goal of salvation of these groups is liberation from oppression.

Professor Glenn Sunshine, whose podcast, *What is Cultural Marxism?* was extremely helpful for the summary above also writes:

> The bottom line here is that for social progress and the liberation of workers to occur, the current culture and value systems must be attacked and replaced by a new one that reflects the interests of the workers, and, more broadly the oppressed. Establishing the new 'truth' is critical to liberation.[2]

Examples could multiply of the impact of these ideas on the West, but the most potent and visible is the trans movement, which added the 't' to the LGB. An early iconic moment was when Bruce Jenner (b. 1949) 'came out' on the front cover of *Vanity Fair* in 2015. Posing as a glamour model with the tag, 'Call me Caitlyn', the world discovered that, although Jenner had been one of America's all-time great male Olympic heroes, 'he had always been a woman'. Sharon James writes:

> This challenge to the man-woman blueprint, which lies at the foundation of family and society is unprecedented.
>
> By 2018 around twenty nations had passed laws affirming the 'right' to 'change sex'– nations including Argentina, Bolivia, Colombia, Denmark, Ecuador, France, Iceland, Ireland, Japan, Malta, Norway, Spain, the United Kingdom, Uruguay, and Vietnam.
>
> In such countries, a man can legally take a female name, and be treated for all legal purposes as a woman (or vice versa). He may be given a new birth certificate. In some of these countries, there is no requirement for such a person to undergo any medical treatment at all (such as hormonal treatment or surgical 'reassignment'). A physically normal man can demand to be recognised as a woman, and demand to freely access women-only facilities (such as swimming pool changing areas or public toilets).[3]

In Scotland, the Scottish National Party (SNP) and the Green Party passed legislation to allow trans women into female prisons and a recent attempt by them to lower the age of consent for reassignment to sixteen with no medical certificates was blocked by the UK government. Gender ideology has affected female world sport with trans women being allowed to compete with women, although there has been a rethink by World Athletics and British cycling. These examples alone show what a powerful impact Gender Ideology, which itself is quite new, is making.

The importance of freedom of speech

Dr Kathleen Stock, who believes trans women are not women, was quoted in *The Telegraph* a few days before taking part in an event at the Oxford Union.

Speaking to the breakfast television show, *Good Morning Britain*, she said:

> We have to have freedom of speech; we have to be able to talk about this. Of course I am causing upset. The position I am fighting against causes a lot of upset. You've got male rapists in female prisons: that causes a lot of upset. You've got children transitioning, doing things to their bodies that they can't take back: that causes upset to their parents. You've got huge numbers of women unable to talk about sex-based rights in their workplaces because they feel stifled: that causes upset.

In a rare intervention into a campus free-speech row, the prime minister told *The Telegraph* that the vocal few must not be allowed to shut down debate and that universities must support, not stifle, contentious discussion.

He said:

> A free society requires free debate. We should all be encouraged to engage respectfully with the ideas of others. University should be an environment where debate is supported, not stifled. We mustn't allow a small but vocal few to shut down discussion. Kathleen Stock's invitation to the Oxford Union should stand.[4]

Knowing the times

When facing such a moment, it is important to step back, think

Christianly and ask 'if we're in a Bonhoeffer ... moment or a Wilberforce moment' states John Stonestreet in another Colson Centre Podcast.[5] The times were bleak in Wilberforce's time in England. The abolition of slavery took forty years of continuous campaigning and, at the time, one in four girls ended up in prostitution from thirteen years of age upwards. Wilberforce fought for the reformation of society under his slogan, 'The Reformation of Manners.' John Stonestreet makes the point that for the faithful Christian it is impossible not to be cultural. Culture is simply what we make of the world and how we order ourselves. The word comes from 'cultivate' in Genesis 2:15, where the Lord, 'took the man and put him in the Garden of Eden to work it and keep it'. We are to be transforming the culture by the impact of our Christian faith. This is what Wilberforce and friends did with remarkable success. Bonhoeffer tried to oppose Hitler, and offered a Christian critique of National Socialism but he was a prophet crying in the wilderness and was executed by the Nazis—yet his influence is still felt.

The jury is still out on what sort of cultural moment we are in, but the Christian consensus is to acknowledge that the centre of Christianity has already passed from the West to the Global South, where most Christians live. We have seen this in the recent Kigali GAFCON conference, mentioned in Chapter 1, but this is true for every living branch of the Church. Incredible growth has occurred in places like China and Africa because they have a supernatural worldview while, in the West, we have succumbed to the prevailing culture where we rely on techniques and experts rather than prayer and the Holy Spirit. The Church in the West has virtually been lost.

The adoption of same-sex blessings by the Church of England is only the latest tragic sign of collapse in the Western Church.

Can the West be re-won for the Gospel of Christ?

Yes, of course it can! God is sovereign in revival and this can happen, even if things look very bleak. All revivals have begun with intense periods of prayer which, before the Reformation, usually began in monasteries and afterwards in covenanted groups such as the Moravians and the Methodist societies. Rod Dreher advocates *The Benedict Option* in his book of that title, which amounts to building a tight-knit, religious community based on the Benedictine principles to ride out the cultural storm, just as the monks did after the fall of the Roman Empire.[6]

I would prefer to look to a spirituality like the Puritans rather than monasteries for inspiration, who were described by J. I. Packer as 'the Lord's Soldier-Pilgrims, just as in Bunyan's Allegory, ... not expecting to be able advance a single step without opposition of one sort or another'.[7] The Puritans lost every battle they fought but had a deep and attractive spirituality that could help sustain the church through the coming storm. They were not the joyless and legalistic people the world would have us believe. Being like the Puritans will help us to be in the world but not of it. This is where transformation over time could come.

What help can we get from 2 Timothy?
2 TIMOTHY 3:1–5 AND ORIGINAL SIN.

> But understand this, that in the last days there will come times of difficulty. For people will be lovers of self, lovers of money, proud,

arrogant, abusive, disobedient to their parents, ungrateful, unholy, heartless, unappeasable, slanderous, without self-control, brutal, not loving good, treacherous, reckless, swollen with conceit, lovers of pleasure rather than lovers of God, having the appearance of godliness, but denying its power. Avoid such people (2 Timothy 3:1–5).

We looked at this section of 2 Timothy in Chapter 5 of this book and noted the link between the last days, which began when Christ arrived on earth, and false teaching and the general increase of evil everywhere, both of which are evidence that the final days have arrived. At this point, I want to put this increase in evil and false teaching in the context of the collapse of Western Culture.

The word, 'difficulty', from verse 1, was used in classical Greek of both dangerous animals and of a stormy sea. This fits my analogy of the coming cultural storm that is undermining Western Culture. From this passage in 2 Timothy 3, are we to think we live in more perilous times for the gospel than any other? Calvin is helpful here:

> Under 'the last days' [v. 1] he [Calvin] includes the universal condition of the Christian Church ... 'For men will be' [v. 2]: It is proper to remark, first, in what he makes the hardship of those 'dangerous' or 'troublesome' times to consist; not in war, nor in famine, nor in diseases, nor in any calamities or inconveniences to which the body is incident, but in the wicked and depraved actions of men.[8]

So, the last days will be like a raging sea, a storm that will be characterized by bad people (all have been tainted by original sin since the Fall—see Genesis 3). Is this present culture any more difficult for the church than previous cultures, since the problem is not bad times but bad people? No, I think not. Ecclesiastes 9:3 says,

'The hearts of the children of man are full of evil, and madness is in their hearts while they live.' This madness just takes different forms in each era.

2 Timothy 3:1 states that the times will be testing throughout the last days. Every generation will have its challenges. In the present times, life is complex and fast moving given its fluid nature. Also, it is hard to make progress with people about the gospel using reason who only relate on an emotional level. That is why prayer and the Holy Spirit become even more important. But there is a common feature of every age. How are bad people transformed? Only by the grace of the Lord Jesus Christ. The gospel is the agent for transformative change, when one person experiences the miracle of new birth and their whole circle of relationships is touched by the power of the supernatural and by the Kingdom of God breaking in.

This is what we need to see under God in the Western Church, but we need to be realistic about human nature and the tendency within the church of 'having the appearance of godliness but denying its power' (v. 5). Sadly, we are seeing false teaching and hypocrisy in the House of Bishops of the Church of England which must be resisted. The answer to this situation is to pray for a spiritual revival and to obey Christ's final command before his ascension in Mathew 28:

> Go therefore and make disciples of all nations, baptizing them in the name of the Father and of the Son and of the Holy Spirit, teaching them to observe all that I have commanded you. And behold, I am with you always, to the end of the age (vv. 19–20).

Is that 'go' command only restricted to the apostles and to those involved in evangelism? Surely, it applies to all faithful Christians who take Christ and his gospel into every area of life including human sexuality, since Christ is Lord of all creation.

As we live in this 'liquid modernity', we have the 'Rock of Ages', Jesus Christ, who declared: 'Heaven and earth will pass away, but my words will not pass away' (Matthew 24:35).

Rock of Ages, cleft for me,
Let me hide myself in Thee;
Let the water and the blood,
From Thy wounded side which flowed,
Be of sin the double cure,
Save from wrath and make me pure.

Not the labours of my hands
Can fulfil Thy law's demands;
Could my zeal no respite know,
Could my tears forever flow,
All for sin could not atone;
Thou must save, and Thou alone.

Nothing in my hand I bring,
Simply to Thy cross I cling;
Naked, come to Thee for dress;
Helpless, look to Thee for grace;
Foul, I to the fountain fly;
Wash me, Saviour, or I die.

While I draw this fleeting breath,
When mine eyes shall close in death,
When I rise to worlds unknown,
And behold Thee on Thy throne,

Rock of Ages, cleft for me,
Let me hide myself in Thee.

(Augustus Toplady, 1740–1778)

A call to faithfulness and engagement

This is not meant as a call for Christians to withdraw but to remember the core of what they believe and live it out in confidence in the Lord and in loving community. We must continue to engage with the culture but be the ark of the Lord floating on the sea (the culture) and not allowing it to leak into the ark (the church), causing it to sink.

In the next chapter, we will attempt to look forward—a risky business since I am neither a prophet nor the son of a prophet! What we can attempt is to try and assess whether this dystopian cultural storm is more like the soft totalitarianism glimpsed by George Orwell in his book, *1984*, or more like the culture described by Aldous Huxley in his book, *Brave New World*. Whatever is coming over the hill, we need to contend for the faith, not by striving in our own strength but standing together in the power of God. Our final chapter (9) will remind us from 2 Timothy 4 that God not man has the last word.

NOTES

1 Dreher, Rod, *The Benedict Option*, p. 40.
2 Sunshine, Glenn, 'Cultural Marxism: Gramsci and the Frankfurt School, Emerging Worldviews 4, 03/11/19. https://breakpoint.org/cultural-marxism-gramsci-and-the-frankfurt-school-emerging-worldviews-4/
3 James, Sharon, 'Gender Ideology: What Christians Need to Know', *Christian Focus*, 2019, p. 17.

4 www.telegraph.co.uk/politics/2023/05/29/universities-free-speech-rishi-sunak-kathleen-stock-oxford/

5 https://breakpoint.org/os-guinness-explains-our-calling-to-this-cultural-moment/

6 Dreher Rod, *The Benedict Option: A Strategy for Christians in a Post-Christian Nation*, (Sentinel, 2017).

7 Packer, J. I., *Among God's Giants*, (Eastbourne: Kingsway Communications, 1991), pp. 24–25.

8 Calvin, John, *Commentary on Timothy, Titus, Philemon*, p. 138. www.biblestudyguide.org/ebooks/comment/calcom43.pdf

8 A dystopian vision of the future

Will the cultural storm be more like the dystopian world imagined by Orwell or by Huxley—state control based on fear or state control based on pleasure and comfort? Will there be physical persecution of the Church? The Reformation involved religious bloodshed in England. Will we see blood on the streets of England again? Historically, persecution of orthodox Christians often comes from the institutional church, using the state to exercise physical violence on what it sees as dissenters and problems.

The godly and courageous Puritans

The Puritan, Richard Baxter (1615–1691) was one of the dissenters ejected from Church of England ministry in 1662. He suffered painful injustices, being put in prison at the age of seventy without a bed to sleep on. John Owen, another sympathetic Puritan (1616–1683), was able to make representations to King Charles II to get Baxter a bed to sleep on. John Bunyan, another Puritan (1628–1688), was imprisoned in Bedford jail because of his refusal to stop preaching when he did not have a licence from the Church of England. It was in 1691, when Baxter died—332 years ago. Could such things happen again in liberal England? Tom Holland has argued that the liberal values of caring for the weak and seeing everyone with equal value comes not from Rome or Athens but from

Christianity. Remove doctrinal Christianity and, in time, you remove its values of tolerance and free speech. This is what is happening in 21st-century England.

We have already noted early on how perilous the situation of the church was as the apostle Paul neared the end of his life and ministry. Commenting on Paul in 2 Timothy, Bishop Moule goes so far as to write, 'that Christianity … trembled humanly speaking, on the verge of annihilation':

> We are so habituated to Christianity as being, apart from its divine character, a vast factor in the modern world that it needs an effort to realize that when this Epistle was written it trembled, humanly speaking, on the verge of annihilation. Did Paul, did Timothy, never half ask themselves if it would not be annihilated? In fact, we may be sure that they did.[1]

Paul is lying chained in prison, deeply concerned about the gospel and its survival as he faces imminent death at the hands of Nero's court. He is wondering whether Timothy is up to the job of holding the line and passing on the faith once received by the saints.

What evidence is there for Bishop Moule's assertion in the text of 2 Timothy?

Was it really that bleak? Firstly, let us look at Paul's concern for Timothy, then at the desertion of key supporters and finally at the turning point in the letter, when Paul realizes that his martyrdom is imminent and, humanly speaking, the Church appears to be too weak to confront the culture of Rome and overcome. Yet, he knows that persecution will not destroy the Church because of the power of God.

1) PAUL'S CONCERN FOR TIMOTHY

We are alerted to the temptation for Timothy to backslide and avoid the inevitable suffering that goes with gospel faithfulness:

Chapter 1, verse 8:

> Therefore, do not be ashamed of the testimony about our Lord, nor of me his prisoner, but share in suffering for the gospel by the power of God,

Chapter 2, verse 3:

> Share in suffering as a good soldier of Christ Jesus.

Chapter 3, verse 12:

> Indeed, all who desire to live a godly life in Christ Jesus will be persecuted,

2) THE DESERTION OF DISCIPLES

Chapter 1, verse 15 is emphatic and painful:

> You are aware that all who are in Asia turned away from me, among whom are Phygelus and Hermogenes.

Chapter 4, verses 9–11:

> Do your best to come to me soon. For Demas, in love with this present world, has deserted me and gone to Thessalonica. Crescens has gone to Galatia, Titus to Dalmatia. Luke alone is with me. Get Mark and bring him with you, for he is very useful to me for ministry.

3) PAUL REALIZES THAT HIS MARTYRDOM IS IMMINENT.

Up until this point Paul thinks he may be released and have further time to strengthen the struggling disciples but, in Chapter 4, verses 6–8, comes the realization of his imminent death:

> For I am already being poured out as a drink offering, and the time of my departure has come. I have fought the good fight, I have finished the race, I have kept the faith. Henceforth there is laid up for me the crown of righteousness, which the Lord, the righteous judge, will award to me on that Day, and not only to me but also to all who have loved his appearing.

As Bishop Moule argues, I think that [Christianity] 'trembled, humanly speaking, on the verge of annihilation' but Paul was supremely confident in the promises and power of God. He believed that the Church would survive and grow in spite of persecution.

Humanly speaking, Christianity faced annihilation with the martyrdom of Paul. It faced annihilation with the fall of the Roman Empire. The Western World based on Christianity is facing another such critical moment. Which way will things go? We must be in the world but not of it. We know that Christ will overcome in the end, but we must understand the times and be better prepared to fight the good fight of faith.

The future: More like Orwell's or Huxley's vision?

Perhaps there will be elements of both dystopian nightmares? Sherelle Jacobs, writing in *The Telegraph* sees soft authoritarianism growing in Britain:

When it comes to freedom, Britain has reached a tipping point. Our country likes to pride itself on being a champion of liberty—the country that bequeathed private property norms, natural rights philosophy and representative government to the United States, leader of the free world.

But after a golden age for liberty that stretches back to the Enlightenment, we are going backwards. Britain's ranking across all manner of global freedom indexes, from academic liberty to online and media freedom, are in freefall. In a spectacular reversal of history, peacetime freedom is now consistently shrinking rather than expanding. Put bluntly, we are sleepwalking into becoming a 'soft authoritarian' outlier in the West.[2]

This 'soft authoritarian' approach was used on ordinary people trying to do the best for their families during the pandemic. *The Telegraph* did an interview of a mother affected:

For lockdown sceptic Molly Kingsley, the discovery that she was spied on by the Government in an attempt to curtail discussion of its controversial coronavirus policies has been nothing short of horrifying.

The mother of two, 44, was disgusted to find out articles she had written for *The Telegraph* cautioning against school closures, the wearing of face masks in classrooms and the vaccination of children had been flagged by the Counter-Disinformation Unit (CDU), set up by ministers to tackle supposed domestic 'threats'.[3]

Big Brother is already watching you!

What follows is another example from *The Telegraph* of censorship by 'Big Brother' government during the Pandemic:

'How secretive units tackling Covid disinformation 'strayed towards censorship.'

The Counter-Disinformation Unit is accused of mission creep by ordering removal of posts that go against government opinions.

Civil servants provided an update on how the national vaccine rollout was being received. There was 'further work to do with decreasing vaccine hesitancy amongst black and minority ethnic communities', and the Government's last-minute decision to change the interval between doses was 'starting to become an area for worries'. This information is recorded in a memo of the meeting, obtained by the Big Brother Watch campaign group under freedom of information laws, and passed to this newspaper …

Somewhat ironically, about a third of the six-page disclosure is so heavily redacted, it comprises pages of black. A section marked 'Key points' is entirely blacked out. So are the names of the individual attendees, other than three civil servants … According to Ms Carlo, there has been huge 'mission creep', and we have arrived at a situation where the Government is effectively policing opinions it disagrees with as 'false' information:

> Whilst everyone would expect the Government and tech giants to act against foreign hostile disinformation campaigns, we should be incredibly cautious about these powers being turned inwards to scan, suppress, and censor the lawful speech of Brits for wrongthink, as is shockingly the case right now.
>
> The very concept of 'wrong information' dictated by a central authority is open to abuse and should be considered far more critically, lest we mirror Chinese-style censorship.[4]

Are we facing a dystopian culture imagined by Orwell and Huxley?

Elements of both visions are happening today, shown by the

quotations above, but which writer makes the more accurate prediction?

> When we compare two versions of dystopia, one is not better than the other. Both are worse but somehow, we have come to accept that a more 'hard' version of dystopia, like Orwell's *1984*, is the one to be feared, whereas the 'soft' form of dystopia as described by Huxley in *Brave New World* is not. This is where, I believe, Huxley was more accurate in his prediction. A futuristic dystopian society won't be one where the government will deploy strict draconian measures to control you but you will live in comfort and happiness all the time and get unused to sadness. As such, you will do everything to be happy all the time, even trade your freedom and thoughts.
>
> Contrary to common belief even among the educated, Huxley and Orwell did not prophesy the same thing. Orwell warns that we will be overcome by an externally imposed oppression. But in Huxley's vision, no Big Brother is required to deprive people of their autonomy, maturity and history. As he saw it, people will come to love their oppression, to adore the technologies that undo their capacities to think.[5]

And that is the key thing from a Christian perspective: the ability to think for ourselves and to have freedom of speech. We live in an irrational age where we have children identifying as animals; Christianity teaches us to think. Attacking the mind and offering an attractive opiate that appeals to hedonism and our desire for security and comfort is a key strategy of the enemy of souls. C. S. Lewis was ahead of his time in recognizing the potency of Satan's devices in the modern age, which the apostle Paul warns us about in

2 Corinthians 2:11: 'so that we would not be outwitted by Satan; for we are not ignorant of his designs'.

The following extended quote, from a site devoted to the work of C. S. Lewis, alerts readers to the urgency, 'to bolster and extend our faith in the face of opposition and deliberate sabotage'.

> Few people in 1947 were writing about demons and their ilk, and still fewer believed in them enough to bother speculating on this question: What if we could see what the temptation of our souls looks like through the eyes of the *other side*? In other words, what if we could interview a demon?
>
> That was Lewis's premise for one of his most durably popular works, perhaps his single most popular work among non-Christian readers; in an ingenious preface, Lewis purports to be beneficiary of the intercepted correspondence of diabolical counsel from a senior devil to an apprentice devil.
>
> Screwtape had actually been published five years earlier ... [it] challenged battle-weary Britons and others around the globe not to give up hope or yield to unbelief in this world, specifically by turning their lively focus on the world to come. In so doing, Lewis established that those only those so heavenly minded have a chance to be of any earthly good.
>
> The story unfolds as a chronological series of letters that captures the downs and ups of Wormwood, Screwtape's nephew, who is trying to use what weapons he has, lies, deceptions, doubts, to undermine the faith of his 'patient', a young man whom we first meet as one struggling to believe, and then who is on and under trial as a new Christian.
>
> As an apologist for Christianity, Lewis used his imagination to seek fresh ways to communicate orthodox Christian faith ...
>
> It is a classic reversal story—that is, it turns upside down our

expectations and affiliations; for example, Satan is reverenced and referenced as 'Our Father Below', while Jesus is termed, simply, 'the Enemy'. By turns comic, sobering, satirical, enlightening, and challenging, Screwtape prepares us to bolster and extend our faith in the face of opposition and deliberate sabotage.[6]

In terms of freedom of speech, the mention of China's invasive surveillance of every citizen by the use of Artificial Intelligence is concerning. Such technology is being used by Western tech companies to gather information on what sells best but could be used by the government to police the state. Already police forces like the Metropolitan force in London have asked for permission to use facial recognition software to help catch criminals. If orthodox Christians are already regarded as 'heretics in the world' (see Vaughan Roberts comments in Chapter 6 of this book), it is only a small step for such heretics to be persecuted because they do not conform to the institutional church or to society's current, acceptable social norms on sexual ethics. Comments by the current Archbishop of Canterbury to seek out ministers for censure who believe that the gospel can bring transformational change through prayer and counselling to same sex attracted people is chilling (See Chapter 5).

The example of government and church in the pandemic

During the pandemic, the UK government went into control mode and so did the Church of England. Given the speed of the impact of Critical Theory[7] and the zealous way it is applied, it is highly likely that Christians, now seen as immoral oppressors over sticking to the Bible's clear teaching on homosexuality, will become increasingly targeted. Already street preachers have been arrested but never charged. Christian teachers, judges and social workers have lost their jobs because of their Christianity. Things are set to get much worse and the Church should prepare itself for physical persecution. Whether the future is more what Orwell or Huxley predicted or a subtle combination of both, times are set to get more challenging for the Church in the West. In the final chapter, we see where our hope comes from as Christians, as we remind ourselves that God—not man, not the state or the unseen powers seeking to draw people away from their Creator and Lord—has the last word on this country and this world.

PSALM 121:1-2

> I lift up my eyes to the hills.
>   From where does my help come?
>   My help comes from the Lord,
>   who made heaven and earth.

NOTES

1 Moule, Bishop Handley C. G., *The Second Epistle to Timothy: Short Devotional Studies on the Dying Letter of St Paul*, (London: The Religious Tract Society, 1906), p. 18. https://biblicalstudies.org.uk/book_2-timothy-devotional-commentary_moule.html

2 www.telegraph.co.uk/news/2023/06/05/covid-mission-creep-just-tip-britains-authoritarian-iceberg/

3 www.telegraph.co.uk/news/2023/06/05/molly-kingsley-interview-covid-19-government-extremist/

4 www.telegraph.co.uk/news/2023/06/02/covid-19-counter-disinformation-policy-forum-censorship

5 https://prabhupant.substack.com/p/orwell-huxley-and-versions-of-dystopia

6 www.cslewis.com/the-devil-and-mr-lewis/

7 'Critical theory today is a diverse phenomenon that draws deeply and variously on strands of Marxist thought, psychoanalysis, feminist, theory, postcolonialism, poststructuralism, queer theory, and deconstruction. It embraces a variety of such approaches and continues to develop its conceptual vocabulary and its range of political concerns. Yet at the core of the various approaches of critical theorists lies a relatively simple set of convictions: the world is to be divided up between those who have power and those who do not; the dominant Western narrative of truth is really an ideological construct designed to preserve the power structure of the status quo; and the goal of critical theory is therefore to destabilize this power structure by destabilizing the dominant narratives that are used to justify—to 'naturalize'—it. Truman, Carl, R., *The Rise and Triumph of the Modern Self*, pp. 225–226.

9 God, not man, has the final word!

I retired from being a parish vicar on 17 May 2022. I preached through 2 Timothy for my final series, and I could not resist entitling my last address as, 'The Time of my Departure has come,' from 2 Timothy 4:6.

Every political career seems to end with failure. (Christian ministry has its political side especially if you serve in the Church of England!) Major policy failure leading to their political demise has been a feature of recent prime ministers: Margaret Thatcher (Poll Tax and divisions over Europe), Tony Blair (Iraq), David Cameron (Brexit). In 2 Timothy 4:9–22, Paul's ministry seems to be heading for disaster and failure. The church has been infiltrated by false teaching.

As I have noted throughout this book, persecution does not destroy the church, but false teaching certainly does. Desertion of key leaders like Demas cast a shadow (v. 10). Verse 11 brings hope since Mark, who had deserted the joint missionary initiative of Paul and Barnabas and led to them parting company, is restored and 'is useful to me for ministry'. Paul has opponents both within the church and outside it: for example, Alexander the coppersmith (v. 14). Desertion is mentioned again in the court case before Caesar: 'all deserted me' (v. 16), which recalls 1:15: 'All who are in Asia turned away from me.' This paints a very bleak picture at the end of Paul's heroic ministry, but the power of God shines through: 'But the Lord stood by me and strengthened me' (2 Timothy 4:17). Those three words are some of the most wonderful in the Bible: 'But the Lord'.

A standing Christian?

The 'Standing Man' analogy from the *Bridge of Spies* film is so encouraging, since this story demonstrates that an ordinary person can do extraordinary things. *Bridge of Spies* is a 2015 film directed by Steven Spielberg. It is the true story of James Donovan (played by Tom Hanks), a lawyer who finds himself thrown into the centre of the Cold War, when the CIA sends him on a near-impossible mission to negotiate the release of a captured American U-2 pilot, Garry Powers, in exchange for a Soviet spy, Rudolf Abel (played by Sir Mark Rylance). Donovan defends Abel and develops a deep respect for him. Abel tells Donavan the story of an otherwise very ordinary man: a friend of his father's struck down by vicious border guards, who keeps getting up repeatedly until the border guards stop beating him. He calls him, 'The Standing Man'. And this is how he sees James Donovan, who experiences the violence of his fellow Americans for being brave enough to be his defence lawyer.

Being able to stand true in exceedingly difficult circumstances is even more possible for ordinary people if we have Christ in us! 'The message might be fully proclaimed', testifies Paul and 'all the Gentiles might hear it. So, I was rescued from the lion's mouth' (v. 17). Paul's confidence in his fellow workers is shaken, but not his confidence in God (v. 18). God will deliver Paul from every evil attack (Ephesians 6:11–12 shows the real battle is not against flesh and blood but unseen spiritual forces) and God sovereignly 'brings [Paul] safely into his heavenly kingdom. To him be the glory for ever and ever. Amen' (v. 18). God, not man, has the final word on Paul and his ministry and that is true for every Christian, whether obscure or well known.

Victorious Christian living

Watchman Nee's commentary on Ephesians has the striking and simple title, *Sit, Walk, Stand* (1974).[1] Paul, in Ephesians, encourages believers to recognize that they sit in the heavenly places with Christ. 'In Christ' is Paul's special phrase for describing the Christian and, in Ephesians 1:20, he describes how God has seated Christ 'at his right hand in the heavenly places'. Hence, Watchman Nee's first word, 'Sit'. This fits with the importance of not striving but resting in Christ, that I have been struggling to do the whole of my Christian life! We are to recognize that the power to live the Christian life comes from being 'in Christ', but we have to 'walk'— the second of Nee's words about the big picture of Ephesians. In Chapter 4, verse 1, Paul says, 'I therefore, a prisoner for the Lord, urge you to walk in a manner worthy of the calling to which you have been called.' Then, in Chapter 6, Paul describes the key to being a Christian Soldier: 'Finally, be strong in the Lord and in the strength of his might,' (v. 10) and, using the powerful metaphor of putting on Christ by putting on armour, he says:

> Therefore, take up the whole armour of God, that you may be able to withstand in the evil day, and having done all, to stand firm. Stand therefore ... (vv. 13–14).

This is *Nee's* third word, 'stand'. Be a standing Christian in the power of Christ, our risen King, who indwells us by the Holy Spirit. Christ living his victorious life through us as we battle not 'against flesh and blood, but … spiritual forces of evil in the heavenly places' (6:12).

One old friend who has witnessed the trials and joys Gloria and I have experienced, commented at the time of my retirement: 'I tell people that the whole of your ministry has been difficult with such varied problems and people, but you have come through.' Looking back over almost forty years of paid Christian ministry, there has been a pattern similar to the situation Paul found himself in at the end of his ministry in 2 Timothy 4. Each job looked as if it would end in failure (vv. 17–18), 'But the Lord stood at my side and gave me strength' (2 Timothy 4:17, NIV). There is this pattern of death and resurrection in Christian ministry. The situation looks bleak, 'but the Lord' makes all the difference and what seemed hopeless becomes hopeful. Jesus gives us this principle of death and resurrection when he states in John 12:24: 'Truly, truly, I say to you, unless a grain of wheat falls into the earth and dies, it remains alone; but if it dies, it bears much fruit.'

As I shared earlier, a big temptation is to strive in our own strength. Paul expresses the biblical balance in Ephesians 6:10: 'Be strong in the Lord' (that is our responsibility) and then he writes, 'and in the strength of his might', (that is God's part). At the start of my Christian life, there was a popular teaching which emphasized God's part at the expense of our part—which instructed us to, 'Let go and let God'. No, we have a part to play; it is a balance. In fact, we can only have victory in Christ if we step up to the plate and exercise faith, by putting on the armour of God and having 'done all, to stand' (Ephesians 6:13). It is through the indwelling Christ working in us and through us that we are to live victorious Christian lives.

Part of that 'standing' is to discern what is going on and play our part. Carl Truman says that the church must wake up to the seriousness of its situation and Rod Dreher says something remarkably similar. Truman and Dreher also agree on Christians in the West holding to the doctrinal teachings of the Bible. The third strand we have seen is the need to build a community of believers who care for one another in practical ways.

Share in suffering as a good soldier of Christ Jesus.

At the start of this book, I said that if something of what is happening across 75% of the Anglican world, i.e., growth alongside persecution, came to the UK then we might see revival. We must prioritise prayer and look to the power of the Holy Spirit, rather than strive in our own flesh—whether that is by relying on techniques of church growth or activism—but simply trust in the Lord and his mighty power. That is not to say that knowledge and activism are not important, but we must get down on our knees and start with God, and then exercise faith and 'stand'. We must be like that 'standing man' spoken of in the film, *Bridge of Spies*. We need to (as a lay reader in my curacy said often to encourage me) 'roll with the punches and keep going forward'.

The world champion heavyweight boxer, Tyson Fury, is a good example of this. He lives in Morecambe, where he trains on the Promenade close to where I live; I met him recently and he autographed for me his book, *Gloves Off*. I gave him and his wife,

Paris, a signed copy of my book, *Marriages are Made in Heaven*, since they are positive examples of a devoted marriage. Great boxers like Tyson need to roll with the punches and like good soldiers, endure discipline.

In this book, we have examined and tried to make sense of the sexual revolution in the Church of England, especially in the last forty years. The huge cultural change means we have to build arks of Christian community, where we can ride out the storm and hold out to others 'the faith once ... delivered to the saints' (Jude 1:3). What have we learnt that may help us to survive and navigate the storm that is coming, which may lead to physical persecution of Christians in England, not seen for hundreds of years? Remember, if physical persecution comes once again to England it will not destroy the Church but build it. The Lord Jesus says, 'Unless a grain of wheat falls into the earth and dies, it remains alone; but if it dies, it bears much fruit' (John 12:24), and, as the early church discovered, 'the blood of the martyrs is the seed'.[2]

An important aspect of Christian hope is the sovereignty of God. The Puritans held a strong belief in this but lost every battle they fought; they were persecuted and many left England to go to America, such as the Pilgrim Fathers. What light may their story hold for present-day orthodox believers in the Church of England facing a coming storm? From the perspective of having forty years ministry in the Church of England, I am not hopeful of its survival in its present form. But what about the Church *in* England? There is a tension, which I mentioned in Chapter 1, between the sovereignty of God and human responsibility. Jesus says, 'I will build my church and the gates of hell shall not prevail against it' (Matthew 16:18), yet that is held in tension with the reality of a weak, erring and at times despairing church.

In the previous chapter, we saw how Bishop Moule strikingly asserted that, when the epistle of 2 Timothy was written, '[the church] trembled, humanly speaking, on the verge of annihilation'. We see this pattern in *The Lord of the Rings Trilogy*, written by an orthodox believer, J. R. R. Tolkien. The mission of the ring bearer appears impossible to accomplish and, repeatedly, it looks like the forces of evil will triumph. Hope seems on the verge of annihilation. Devin Brown, Professor of English at Asbury University and the author of the book, *A Life Observed: A Spiritual Biography of C.S. Lewis*, wrote a fascinating article entitled, 'Is the Lord of the Rings Christian?' He quotes, John Piper:

> In his recent book, *Providence*, John Piper notes that in reference to God, the word providence has come to mean 'the act of purposefully providing for, or sustaining and governing, the world'.[3] He suggests that another way to express what we mean by God's providence is to say that God 'sees to it that things happen in a certain way'. Both ways of speaking about how divine providence works in our world also apply to Middle-earth ...
>
> In Middle-earth, as in our world, the workings of providence are typically veiled, making them sometimes discernible only in hindsight. In words that briefly pull back this veil, Gandalf concludes, 'Bilbo was meant to find the Ring, and not by its maker. In which case you also were meant to have it.'[4] Here, Gandalf uses the passive voice without specifying who or what it was that intended these events to take place, thus implying the work of divine providence in a way similar to the person who says, 'God had a plan. We were meant to meet that day.'[5]

God has a plan for the world, and he is working it out. This plan is centred on Christ and his Church, and it will not be thwarted. Just as in the story of *The Lord of the Rings*, God's work in building his Church, 'trembled, humanly speaking, on the verge of annihilation', when Paul was about to be martyred by Nero, but the words and promise of Jesus that 'heaven and earth will pass away but my words will not pass away' (Matt. 24:35), were vindicated once more and will be again and again until he comes for his bride. As Piper puts it, divine providence means that God 'sees to it that things happen in a certain way'. As Devin Brown suggests, 'the workings of providence are typically veiled, making them sometimes discernible only in hindsight.' Looking back over forty years of marriage to Gloria, I can trace divine providence. I wrote about this in my last book, *Marriages are Made in Heaven* (2021).[6] Looking back over forty years of Christian ministry in the Church of England, with all the struggles, opposition, and disappointments, I can trace the providence of God spreading his Word, bringing salvation in Christ, and answering prayer and building his Church.

God, not man, has the last word.

Today it looks bleak for the Church in the West but there is hope in the gospel and in the history of the church through the ages. We have seen similar types of cultural moments before. The Roman Empire tried to destroy the Church and it looked bleak as Paul prepared to leave planet earth. The Church survived persecution and grew. We see it again in the great cultural moment when the Roman Empire fell. Augustine thought Christ must come at that point since it was so catastrophic. He did not; but the Church survived the storm and flourished.

We do not know what is coming over the hill, but we know through the evidence of the Scriptures, church history and our experience of strength in weakness, the truth of those wonderful words in 2 Timothy 4:17: 'But the Lord'. We must reject 'jellyfish Christianity', attractive though it seems—as is said *Brave New World*, 'Christianity without tears'.[7] Instead, as good soldiers of Christ we must endure suffering and march forwards towards heaven, living our lives to the glory of God whatever happens. One of the key principles in Scripture is the hope of heaven. This is how clergyman, William Fullerton, in 1917 approached his sixtieth birthday and his official retirement (clearly life expectancy is one of the things that is different today), giving his view of rest and service:

> It has been said that in a well-ordered human story sixty years should be given to service, and the seventh decade should be the Sabbath of life. But my rest must be in further service. So, I but pause awhile at the milestone to remember all the way the Lord has led me, to brace myself for the rest of the journey; and then *greeting* with a braver heart and a blither step to trudge on. There is a turn in the road in front of me and I do not know what may be round the corner, but I can say 'Heaven's ahead, Hurrah!'[8]

NOTES

1 Nee, Watchman, *Sit, Walk, Stand*, (Fort Washington, PA: Christian Literature Crusade, 1974).

2 Tertullian, www.brainyquote.com/quotes/tertullian_154818. Sourced: 20/07/24

3 Piper, John, *Providence*, (Wheaton, Illinois: Crossway, 2021), p. 30.

Chapter 9

4 Tolkien, J. R. R., *The Lord of the Rings: 50th Anniversary, One Vol. Edition*, (Mariner Books, 2005), p. 56.

5 Brown, Devin, 'Is "Lord of the Rings" Christian?' January 3, 2022. www.desiringgod.org/articles/is-lord-of-the-rings-christian

6 Donald, Steve, *Marriages are Made in Heaven*, (Welwyn Garden City: Evangelical Press, 2021).

7 www.huxley.net/bnw/seventeen.html

8 William Fullerton [1857–1932], *At the Sixtieth Milestone Incidents of the Journey*, (London, Edinburgh & New York: Marshall Brothers Ltd, 1917), pp. 7–8.

Postscript

L et me bring you up to date with three significant developments in the evangelical opposition to the direction of travel by the majority of Church of England bishops on the issue of same-sex blessings and gay marriage of clergy. Evangelicals within the Church of England have taken measures to try and differentiate themselves from the mainly liberal House of Bishops and seek some sort of restructuring that would allow them to continue with integrity in the Church of England. Firstly, there is a recent article by John Dunnett in Evangelicals Now in June 2024. He is the National Director of the Church of England Evangelical Council (CEEC). Secondly, the CEEC have established the Ephesian Fund, which is a way of channelling evangelical monies to orthodox parishes. I have copied material from the CEEC website to show how this Ephesian Fund is set up and its purpose. And thirdly, there is a letter by a very significant evangelical group called 'Alliance' on 26 June 2024 to the two Archbishops of the Church of England stating that the adoption of the 'Living in Love and Faith' project, i.e., same-sex blessings and the marriage of same-sex clergy (on the agenda for discussion at the July 2024 General Synod) would lead to the formation of a parallel Province.

* * *

John Dunnett in *Evangelicals Now* June 2024

THE URGENT NEED FOR A C OF E 'SETTLEMENT': KEY QUESTIONS

Following the most recent Church of England General Synod, it was announced that three groups would take forward the work of the 'Living in Love and Faith' (LLF) project relating to prayers for same sex couples, and would be overseen by a programme board, chaired by the Archbishop of York.

These three working groups are looking at pastoral guidance, the introduction of standalone 'Prayers of Love and Faith' and charged with proposing provisions or a 'settlement', as deemed necessary.

The concept of 'settlement' raises different questions for different constituencies. Many liberals are asking why anything further than the freedom not to use the LLF prayers is needed. For those of us who wish to hold onto a historic, Anglican and Biblical understanding, the question is why would others not want to offer a settlement that secures our position in the Church of England, and which might help, to some degree at least, to secure the unity of which the bishops continually speak?

Within our own constituency, people have raised a number of questions around settlement—which this article addresses:

1. SHOULD WE JUST 'HOLD OUR GROUND' AND PRAY?

Some have suggested that our focus should not be on advocating settlement, rather on 'holding our ground' and praying that God will restore and revive His Church. This is, of course, a prayer that I imagine most of us would subscribe to. At the same time, we should not discount the possibility that God is working to revive and refine His Church through such a settlement. And I'm not sure that a commitment to pray for revival discounts the necessity of institutional engagement and rearrangement.

2. LET'S NOT WORRY, IT WOULD BE ILLEGAL TO CHANGE THE DOCTRINE OF MARRIAGE, WOULDN'T IT?

Some in our constituency are quite rightly pointing out the legal and theological challenges to the aspirations of the House of Bishops to introduce the standalone services and make it possible for clergy to marry same-sex partners. It is clear to most people that this does in effect change the doctrine of marriage within the Church of England and ride roughshod over good synodical process. However, the sad reality is that it appears that, despite being aware of this, the House of Bishops has a mind to driving this forward. And if it's true that 'where there's a will, there's a way', then I imagine the House of Bishops will find a way to justify their aspirations to themselves and sanction a course of action that they feel will be defensible. In practice, it would be possible to allow clergy to marry a same-sex partner by not implementing the same disciplinary procedures that might be expected of them, rather than by actively pursuing a change in the doctrine of marriage. In practice, the end result is the same, though the House of Bishops may choose to deny this.

3. THE IDEA OF 'SETTLING' SUGGESTS ENABLING SPACE FOR LIBERALISM, AND I CAN'T SUPPORT THAT!

Some in our constituency are nervous about the idea of 'settlement' because they believe in good conscience that they are not able to support in any way a proposal that defends or makes space for liberalism. The conscience of these brothers and sisters must be recognised, but at the same time we have to face the reality that we might be having to choose not between good and bad, but between the lesser of two evils. If the choice is between the doctrine of the whole of the Church of the England changing, or differentiating in such a way that part of the Church of England retains its Biblical doctrine, then a vote for settlement might be a vote for orthodoxy.

4. WE SHOULD HOLD ON UNTIL THE NEXT GENERAL SYNOD ELECTIONS— WE'LL WIN MORE SEATS.

Finally, some are encouraging us to 'hold the ground' until the next General Synod election at which point we can gain control of the Synod. Speaking as someone who has been on General Synod since 2005, and currently chair of EGGS (Evangelical Group on General Synod)—the largest group in Synod—it is my view that this is wishful thinking and, though I would welcome it, I do not believe even our best effort would give us the voting 'power' in dioceses to achieve this end.

Readers will be aware that other Provinces in the Anglican Communion have already liberalised their ethics around sex and marriage (see 'Learning from Elsewhere'—available to watch on the Church of England Evangelical Council's website). There are obviously a number of lessons that we can learn from the experience of others, but these would include the need to pursue settlement, rather than find ourselves being 'boiled in the proverbial pan'.

Our hope in pursuing settlement is that it would guarantee

orthodoxy a secure base within the Church of England for the future. The statistics suggest that the current growth in the Church of England can be found primarily in evangelical churches—and such a secure base would thereby provide the starting point for growth going forward. God willing, this could be a base from which the orthodoxy of the Church of England could be re-established. A different question always needs to be asked: 'What happens if we don't get an acceptable settlement?' But that's another article...[1]

(Used with permission from CEEC)

* * *

What is the Ephesian Fund?

Strap line: Fuelling orthodox evangelical Anglican ministry across England.

Evangelicals have always given generously to support the life and witness of local churches. However, the decision of the House of Bishops to walk away from a historic biblical understanding of sex and marriage is causing many evangelicals to review their giving to the Church of England.

If, in good conscience, you feel unable to continue personally giving to your bishop(s)/diocese via your PCC, the Ephesian Fund provides an alternative and is designed to help your giving go to local churches that are committed to biblical faith. The Ephesian Fund also provides PCCs with a way to give their parish share to the diocese in support of similar churches.[2]

Orthodox group 'Alliance' letter to the archbishops, 26 June 2024, carries the threat of forming a parallel Province if LLF goes ahead.

This coming together of such a broad orthodox coalition amounts to a serious structural split in the Church of England. It is significant not in terms of numbers of clergy (Alliance quotes 2,000) but in the groups represented. These are significant players including *The Alpha group* which was started by Nicky Gumbel at Holy Trinity Brompton and *New Wine* which represents Anglican Charismatics as well as those under the umbrella of the Church of England Evangelical Council (CEEC). It is also significant that the letter was released in coordination with the eleven dissenting bishops of the Church of England who are publicly opposed to LLF. This marks a serious turning point.

The Alliance Group writes,

> Dear Archbishop Justin and Archbishop Stephen,
> We write as a broad coalition of leaders of networks across different traditions supported by more than 2,000 clergy within the Church of England. We have read the orthodox bishops' statement published earlier today and wholeheartedly agree and support them in their endeavours to remain faithful to the orthodox teaching of the Church of England.
> The authors of the Alliance letter warn:
> If the further departure from the Church's doctrine suggested by the Synod papers does go ahead, we will have no choice but rapidly to establish what would in effect be a new de facto 'parallel Province' within the Church of England and to seek pastoral oversight from bishops who remain faithful to orthodox teaching on marriage and

sexuality. We will encourage all church leaders who are in sympathy with The Alliance to join the parallel Province.

We will take action with immediate effect to open up a new pre-ordination stream for potential ordinands, in partnership with orthodox bishops, to reverse the decline caused in part by this unconstitutional and unorthodox process.

We are not leaving the Church of England or the Anglican Communion. We wish to stay loyal to the one holy catholic and apostolic Church throughout the world rather than be part of a schismatic move which departs from the teaching received and upheld not only by the vast majority of the Anglican Communion (representing around 75% of the Anglican Communion's 80 million members), the Roman Catholic Church, the Orthodox Churches but also the vast majority of other churches around the world.[3]

This letter by the 'Alliance' is a remarkable development.
Will it be enough to stop this liberal drift? It will give many of the bishops supporting these unscriptural proposals pause for thought, but I do not think it will stop it. This was shown by the vote in General Synod on 4 July 2024, reported by *The Telegraph*. Cameron Henderson wrote:

The Church of England has taken its first steps towards allowing gay members of the clergy to marry. The General Synod, the Church's legislative body, voted to pass proposals that pave the way towards a report on the question of same-sex civil marriage ceremonies between members of the clergy or one member of the clergy and a lay person.[4]

How this new parallel Province (in effect a third non-geographical Province alongside Canterbury in the south and York in the north) will work in practice raises considerable problems of implementation. If the present legal structures remain, how will orthodox clergy be licenced when they start in new parishes? How will the eleven existing orthodox bishops cope with all the extra pastoral oversight on top of work in their own diocese? I would guess the 'Alliance group' behind this letter have thought about these problems. I would imagine the answer would be to consecrate more clergy as bishops.

I would predict that if this parallel Province is set up there will be massive chaos, and in the event of such chaos the archbishops and the General Synod may be forced into making structural change to bring order to a very messy situation. I am guessing that this may well be the strategy of the 'Alliance group'. It does seem, from the vote in General Synod in July reported by *The Telegraph*, that LLF is going ahead. The encouragement for evangelicals is the growing courage and unity of those represented by 'The Alliance group', including bishops, clergy and laity who have drawn a line in the sand. It now seems inevitable that there will be a major split in the Church of England.

NOTES

1 https://www.e-n.org.uk/comment/2024-06-the-urgent-need-for-a-cofe-settlement-key-questions/. Sourced: 26/07/24.
2 www.ephesianfund.org.uk/
3 https://anglican.ink/wp-content/uploads/2024/06/Letter-7-to-Archbishops-26-06-24.pdf
4 www.telegraph.co.uk/news/2024/07/08/church-of-england-votes-to-allow-gay-clergy-to-marry/

Glossary of terms

Anglican Communion: It used to be quite simple, in meaning those Provinces of the Church of England in fellowship with the Archbishop of Canterbury. But now there is GAFCON (see below) and The Global South (see below). These represent 75% of Anglicans worldwide, which consists of 80 million believers. After the acceptance of same-sex blessings by the Archbishop of Canterbury (ABC) there are calls from many dissenting Provinces to no longer see the ABC as the de-factor head of the Anglican Communion.

Athanasius (AD 298–373) was a bishop of Alexandria (Egypt), in the 4th century. He is recognized as a great leader and doctor of the early church by Protestants.

AMiE is an Anglican convocation (equivalent to a diocese) affiliated to the Anglican Network in Europe (ANIE) that seeks to establish Anglican Churches in England outside the Church of England. It was created with the support of the Global Anglican Future Conference (GAFCON) and is part of the Anglican realignment.

ANiE is a small Christian denomination in the Anglican tradition with churches in Europe (primarily in England). Formed as part of the worldwide Anglican realignment, it is a member jurisdiction of the Global Fellowship of Confessing Anglicans (GAFCON) and is under the primatial oversight of the chairman of the GAFCON Primates Council. GAFCON recognizes ANiE as a 'proto Province'. AMiE is an Anglican convocation part of ANiE.

The Benedict Option 2017: Book by Rod Dreher. 'The most discussed and important religious book of the decade.' David Brooks, *The New York Times*.

Canons of the Church of England are the legal framework of the denomination. It helps Anglicans to express a shared identity through worship by reminding them to use only authorized forms of service. It also expresses the doctrine of the church. The most important canon is Canon A5 (1969) which states that the doctrine of the Church of England is grounded in the Holy Scriptures, and in such teachings of the ancient Fathers and Councils of the Church as are agreeable to the said Scriptures. In particular such doctrine is to be found in the Thirty-nine Articles of Religion, the Book of Common Prayer and the Ordinal.

Church Provincial Structures in England: The Church of England legally is made up of two Provinces, Canterbury and York, covering forty-two dioceses. Each diocese is split into deaneries and parishes.

Canterbury Communion: Provinces within the Anglican Communion who still look for leadership of some sort from the Archbishop of Canterbury.

Confessing Church: Orthodox bible-believing Christians.

Differentiation: In the context of opposition to the introduction of same-sex blessings, these are parishes who want to distance themselves, usually by withholding parish share and by nonattendance at deanery and diocesan synods. In the Diocese of London, a new parallel 'chapter' of evangelical clergy has been set up. Clergy unhappy with the innovation of same-sex blessings can attend this instead of chapters run by the diocese.

Dystopia: An imaginary place or condition in which everything is as bad as possible as opposed to the perfection of utopia.

Ecumenism: (noun) refers to a movement or effort promoting unity among Christian churches or denominations. In a more general sense, it may also refer to movements promoting worldwide unity among the various religions through greater cooperation and improved understanding. The idea is normally expressed in its adjective form, ecumenical, in terms such as 'ecumenical thinking', 'ecumenical activities', or 'the ecumenical movement'.

GAFCON: Global Anglican Futures Conference. First held in 2008 in Jerusalem in response to the consecration of the first gay bishop in 2005. GAFCON was created to guard and proclaim biblical truth globally and provide fellowship for orthodox Anglicans.

Global South: Provinces of the Anglican Communion who wish to reboot and reform the worldwide Anglican Communion.

General Synod: the Parliament of the Church of England that makes its laws for governing its diocese, deaneries and parishes and clergy and laity. It also oversees its policies regarding the use of its monies and assets.

House of Bishops: One of three houses in General Synod who represent the bishops.

Irregular Action: Acts that would be deemed against the rules of the Church of England but in line with the teaching of Scripture, Reason and Tradition. For example, inviting an outside bishop to take a confirmation service when a diocese presents a heterodox[1] bishop, or cutting parish share in order to fund mission.

Jerusalem Declaration: Theological principles for a radical realignment of worldwide Anglican belief and practice.

Lambeth Conference: A meeting every ten years at Lambeth of clergy, bishops and laity of the Anglican Communion.

Liberal Progressives: Liberal in the sense of having a low view of Scripture and a high view of human reason. Progressive in the sense of wanting to leave behind accepted ideas and try modern ones.

LLF (Living in Love and Faith): A five-year engagement of the wide divergent views on human sexuality within the Church of England. This prepared the way for the acceptance of gay blessings at the February 2023 General Synod. The bishops in favour are working out 'pastoral accommodation' for those opposed, after declining the idea of a Third Province for those against these radical changes.

Provinces: National churches within Anglicanism worldwide. England is divided into two Provinces: Canterbury for southern diocese and York for northern ones.

Revisionist Theologies: Liberal Progressives who wish to revise the accepted interpretation of Scripture.

Third Province: A non-geographical Province with its own separate bishops, canons and theological training, separate from Canterbury and York Provinces.

Woke: Woke is now defined in the dictionary as 'aware of and actively attentive to important facts and issues (especially issues of racial and social justice),' and identified as U.S. slang. It originated in African American English and gained more widespread use beginning in 2014 as part of the Black Lives Matter movement. By the end of that same decade, it was also being applied by some as a general pejorative for anyone who is or appears to be politically left-leaning.[2]

NOTES

1 The term heterodox simply means 'any opinions or doctrines at variance with the official or orthodox position." [1]. Used in contrast to orthodoxy, it is synonymous with the term "unorthodox" and is even closely tied to the word, " heresy". https://www.theopedia.com/heterodox

2 www.merriam-webster.com/wordplay/woke-meaning-origin